S0-AFH-392

# Well
# Worth
# Saving

―――――――

**Markets and Governments in Economic History**

A SERIES EDITED BY PRICE FISHBACK

Also in the series:

The Charleston Orphan House: Children's Lives
in the First Public Orphanage in America
by John Murray

The Institutional Revolution: Measurement and
the Economic Emergence of the Modern World
by Douglas W. Allen


**NBER Series on Long-Term Factors in Economic Development**

A National Bureau of Economic Research Series

EDITED BY CLAUDIA GOLDIN

Also in the series:

Robert William Fogel, Enid M. Fogel, Mark Guglielmo, and Nathaniel Grotte
Political Arithmetic: Simon Kuznets and the Empirical Tradition in Economics
(University of Chicago Press, 2013)

Stanley L. Engerman and Kenneth L. Sokoloff
Economic Development in the Americas since 1500: Endowments and Institutions
(Cambridge University Press, 2012)

Roderick Floud, Robert W. Fogel, Bernard Harris, and Sok Chul Hong
The Changing Body: Health, Nutrition, and Human Development in the Western World
since 1700 (Cambridge University Press, 2011)

# Well Worth Saving

HOW THE

NEW DEAL

SAFEGUARDED

HOME OWNERSHIP

PRICE FISHBACK,

JONATHAN ROSE,

AND

KENNETH SNOWDEN

THE UNIVERSITY

OF CHICAGO PRESS

Chicago and London

**Price Fishback** is the Thomas R. Brown Professor of Economics at the University of Arizona and a research associate of the National Bureau of Economic Research. He is the author or editor of several books, including *A Prelude to the Welfare State* and *Government and the American Economy*, both also published by the University of Chicago Press. **Jonathan Rose** is an economist with the Federal Reserve Board of Governors. **Kenneth Snowden** is associate professor of economic history at the University of North Carolina at Greensboro and a research associate of the National Bureau of Economic Research.

The University of Chicago Press, Chicago 60637
The University of Chicago Press, Ltd., London
© 2013 by The University of Chicago
All rights reserved. Published 2013.
Printed in the United States of America

22  21  20  19  18  17  16  15  14  13      1  2  3  4  5

ISBN-13: 978-0-226-08244-8     (cloth)
ISBN-13: 978-0-226-08258-5     (e-book)

DOI: 10.7208/chicago/9780226082585.001.0001

Library of Congress Cataloging-in-Publication Data

Fishback, Price Van Meter.
    Well worth saving: how the New Deal safeguarded home ownership / Price Fishback, Jonathan Rose, and Kenneth Snowden.
        pages; cm. — (Markets and governments in economic history)
    Includes bibliographical references and index.
    ISBN 978-0-226-08244-8 (cloth: alkaline paper) — ISBN 978-0-226-08258-5 (e-book)   1. Home Owners' Loan Corporation — History.   2. Mortgage loans — United States — History — 20th century.   3. Home ownership — United States — History — 20th century.   4. New Deal, 1933 –1939.   I. Rose, Jonathan Derek. II. Snowden, Kenneth A.   III. Title.   IV. Series: Markets and governments in economic history.
    HG3729.U5F57 2013
    332.7′220973 — dc23                                    2013015699

♾ This paper meets the requirements of ANSI/NISO Z39.48-1992 (Permanence of Paper).

## NBER Board of Directors: Listed by Affiliation
September 24, 2012

### Officers

Kathleen B. Cooper, *Chairman*
Martin B. Zimmerman, *Vice Chairman*
James M. Poterba, *President and Chief*
*Executive Officer*
Robert Mednick, *Treasurer*

Kelly Horak, *Controller and Assistant*
*Corporate Secretary*
Alterra Milone, *Corporate Secretary*
Gerardine Johnson, *Assistant Corporate*
*Secretary*

### Directors at Large

Peter C. Aldrich
Elizabeth E. Bailey
John H. Biggs
John S. Clarkeson
Don R. Conlan
Kathleen B. Cooper
Charles H. Dallara
George C. Eads
Jessica P. Einhorn

Mohamed El-Erian
Linda Ewing
Jacob A. Frenkel
Judith M. Gueron
Robert S. Hamada
Peter Blair Henry
Karen N. Horn
John Lipsky
Laurence H. Meyer

Michael H. Moskow
Alicia H. Munnell
Robert T. Parry
James M. Poterba
John S. Reed
Marina v. N. Whitman
Martin B. Zimmerman

### Directors by University Appointment

George Akerlof, *California, Berkeley*
Jagdish Bhagwati, *Columbia*
Timothy Bresnahan, *Stanford*
Alan V. Deardorff, *Michigan*
Ray C. Fair, *Yale*
Franklin Fisher, *Massachusetts Institute*
*of Technology*
Edward Foster, *Minnesota*

John P. Gould, *Chicago*
Mark Grinblatt, *California, Los Angeles*
Bruce Hansen, *Wisconsin–Madison*
Marjorie B. McElroy, *Duke*
Joel Mokyr, *Northwestern*
Andrew Postlewaite, *Pennsylvania*
Uwe E. Reinhardt, *Princeton*
David B. Yoffie, *Harvard*

### Directors by Appointment of Other Organizations

Bart van Ark, *The Conference Board*
Christopher Carroll, *American Statistical*
*Association*
Jean-Paul Chavas, *Agricultural and Applied*
*Economics Association*
Martin Gruber, *American Finance Association*
Ellen L. Hughes-Cromwick, *National*
*Association for Business Economics*
Thea Lee, *American Federation of Labor*
*and Congress of Industrial Organizations*

William W. Lewis, *Committee for Economic*
*Development*
Robert Mednick, *American Institute of*
*Certified Public Accountants*
Alan L. Olmstead, *Economic History Association*
Peter L. Rousseau, *American Economic*
*Association*
Gregor W. Smith, *Canadian Economics*
*Association*

### Directors Emeriti

Glen G. Cain
Carl F. Christ
George Hatsopoulos
Saul H. Hymans

Lawrence R. Klein
Rudolph A. Oswald
Peter G. Peterson
Nathan Rosenberg

John J. Siegfried
Craig Swan

## Relation of the Directors to the
## Work and Publications of the
## National Bureau of Economic Research

1. The object of the NBER is to ascertain and present to the economics profession, and to the public more generally, important economic facts and their interpretation in a scientific manner without policy recommendations. The Board of Directors is charged with the responsibility of ensuring that the work of the NBER is carried on in strict conformity with this object.

2. The President shall establish an internal review process to ensure that book manuscripts proposed for publication DO NOT contain policy recommendations. This shall apply both to the proceedings of conferences and to manuscripts by a single author or by one or more co-authors but shall not apply to authors of comments at NBER conferences who are not NBER affiliates.

3. No book manuscript reporting research shall be published by the NBER until the President has sent to each member of the Board a notice that a manuscript is recommended for publication and that in the President's opinion it is suitable for publication in accordance with the above principles of the NBER. Such notification will include a table of contents and an abstract or summary of the manuscript's content, a list of contributors if applicable, and a response form for use by Directors who desire a copy of the manuscript for review. Each manuscript shall contain a summary drawing attention to the nature and treatment of the problem studied and the main conclusions reached.

4. No volume shall be published until forty-five days have elapsed from the above notification of intention to publish it. During this period a copy shall be sent to any Director requesting it, and if any Director objects to publication on the grounds that the manuscript contains policy recommendations, the objection will be presented to the author(s) or editor(s). In case of dispute, all members of the Board shall be notified, and the President shall appoint an ad hoc committee of the Board to decide the matter; thirty days additional shall be granted for this purpose.

5. The President shall present annually to the Board a report describing the internal manuscript review process, any objections made by Directors before publication or by anyone after publication, any disputes about such matters, and how they were handled.

6. Publications of the NBER issued for informational purposes concerning the work of the Bureau, or issued to inform the public of the activities at the Bureau, including but not limited to the NBER Digest and Reporter, shall be consistent with the object stated in paragraph 1. They shall contain a specific disclaimer noting that they have not passed through the review procedures required in this resolution. The Executive Committee of the Board is charged with the review of all such publications from time to time.

7. NBER working papers and manuscripts distributed on the Bureau's web site are not deemed to be publications for the purpose of this resolution, but they shall be consistent with the object stated in paragraph 1. Working papers shall contain a specific disclaimer noting that they have not passed through the review procedures required in this resolution. The NBER's web site shall contain a similar disclaimer. The President shall establish an internal review process to ensure that the working papers and the web site do not contain policy recommendations, and shall report annually to the Board on this process and any concerns raised in connection with it.

8. Unless otherwise determined by the Board or exempted by the terms of paragraphs 6 and 7, a copy of this resolution shall be printed in each NBER publication as described in paragraph 2 above.

As a further and urgently necessary step in the program to promote economic recovery, I ask the Congress for legislation to protect small home owners from foreclosure and to relieve them of a portion of the burden of excessive interest and principal payments incurred during the period of higher values and higher earnings power.

Implicit in the legislation which I am suggesting to you is a declaration of national policy. This policy is that the broad interests of the nation require that special safeguards should be thrown around home ownership as a guaranty of social and economic stability, and that to protect home owners from inequitable enforced liquidation, in a time of general distress, is a proper concern of the Government.

The legislation I propose follows the general lines of the farm mortgage refinancing bill. The terms are such as to impose the least possible charge upon the national Treasury consistent with the objects sought. It provides machinery through which existing mortgage debts on small homes may be adjusted to a sound basis of values without injustice to investors, at substantially lower interest rates and with provision for postponing both interest and principal payments in cases of extreme need.

The resources to be made available through a bond issue, to be guaranteed as to interest only by the Treasury, will, it is thought, be sufficient to meet the needs of those to whom other methods of financing are not available.

At the same time the plan of settlement will provide a standard which should put an end to present uncertain and chaotic conditions that create fear and despair among both home owners and investors.

Legislation of this character is a subject that demands our most earnest, thoughtful and prompt consideration.

— Message from President Roosevelt to Congress, April 13, 1933

# Contents

# Preface

In 2008, the Home Owners' Loan Corporation (HOLC) was in the news for the first time in half a century. The HOLC was a New Deal program created in 1933 to respond to the Depression-era mortgage crisis, and with the advent of a new crisis in 2007, politicians from all parts of the spectrum believed it to be an informative precedent for new legislation. Barack Obama reviewed the history: "Roosevelt purchased a whole bunch of homes. Over time, home values went back up, and in fact [the] government made a profit." Hillary Clinton stated, "I've proposed a new Home Owners' Loan Corporation," and John McCain suggested something similar: "I would order the secretary of the treasury to immediately buy up the bad home loan mortgages in America and renegotiate at the new value of those homes." Economists agreed that policy makers should learn from the HOLC's history. Robert Shiller, of Yale University, noted that "[i]n the short run, a new institution modeled on the old Home Owners' Loan Corporation of the 1930s would go far in helping to shore up confidence in the mortgage market." Alan Blinder, of Princeton University, called for a revival: "It is said that history never repeats itself. But sometimes there are sequels. Now is the time to re-establish the Incredible HOLC."[1]

Remarkably, seven decades after the HOLC's creation, there were no readily available answers to some fundamental questions about the program. To those pondering the HOLC in 2008, it was not immediately apparent how the HOLC had successfully obtained such a large size—having refinanced roughly one-fifth of the nation's nonfarm home mortgages—nor was it clear exactly how the HOLC interacted with borrowers and lenders. There were deeper questions as well, such as whether the HOLC contributed to the recovery of housing and mortgage markets. And there was a claim that the HOLC had turned a profit, repeated every time the HOLC was discussed (or so it seemed). Moreover, much was unknown about the background to the HOLC, including the broader history of real estate and mortgage finance between the two world wars.[2]

This monograph provides the first modern, comprehensive analysis of the HOLC that gathers in one place all that we and others have learned about the HOLC over the past several years. In this effort, the authors owe a large intellectual debt to C. Lowell Harriss, whose 1951 study, *History and Policies of the*

*Home Owners' Loan Corporation*, is an invaluable documentary guide to HOLC operations and laid the foundation for this book. Our work does not supplant Harriss's but rather adds to it with analysis of important unanswered questions about the HOLC, such as those raised in the previous paragraph.

Over the past several years, the three of us (through independent research projects) have assembled new databases from printed, mimeographed, and microfilmed HOLC records and employed modern statistical and theoretical tools to investigate important unanswered questions about the HOLC. Rose, for example, uncovered the sample of loans that had been collected by Harriss, which had been microfilmed and placed in a box stored on the Upper East Side of Manhattan for decades. In an analysis outlined in chapter 7, Rose used the data to describe how the HOLC often accommodated lenders when balancing the need to secure the participation of those lenders with the desire to give principal reductions to borrowers. Two groups of researchers—Fishback with Alfonso Flores-Lagunes, William Horrace, Shawn Kantor, and Jaret Treber; and Snowden with Charles Courtemanche—used more standard policy evaluation tools to assess the HOLC's impact during the mid- and late 1930s on home ownership, housing prices, and new home construction. Independently, both groups of researchers assembled data sets covering HOLC activity in every county of the United States and, through analyses that are described in chapter 9, reached similar conclusions. The HOLC improved prices and home ownership, but not enough to completely reverse the damage to both that occurred during the mortgage crisis.

These three research projects ended in articles published in academically oriented economic journals. After completing these independent studies, we worried that leaving our published research findings in academic journals would make that knowledge inaccessible to a general audience. We also realized that we had learned much more about the HOLC and its era than we had been able to include in those articles, and did not want those findings to be lost, as knowledge about the HOLC had been lost in the past. While two chapters in this book contain versions of our prior work, the rest represent additional analysis that pulls together a wide variety of sources, including dusty volumes and government reports published in the 1930s, 1940s, and 1950s; contemporary press accounts of the HOLC; and the documentary history of the program as it was recorded in correspondence, operations manuals, and other mimeographed, carbon-copied, handwritten, and published documents that are held in the National Archives.

In sum, our published research is summarized in chapters 7 and 9, while the rest of this book covers important aspects of the HOLC and its era that we believe are not well known at this point by anyone except us. We begin in chapter 1 by using the actual stories of several HOLC borrowers to introduce the program and by summarizing our principal results. From there, the book is laid out in four parts.

The first part provides the context for the HOLC. We characterize, in chapter 2, the institutions and contracts that defined mortgage finance in the 1920s, an era with a booming housing market and a corresponding expansion of mortgage debt. As described in chapter 3, the mortgage finance market was in deep crisis by 1933 despite previous attempts to unwind its problems at the state and federal levels over the previous four years. The continued crisis prompted a broad public consensus behind the HOLC Act's passage, as summarized in chapter 4. This part of the book concludes with chapter 5, which examines the rationale for the HOLC from the public policy perspective that economists use to assess such market interventions.

The second part of the book consists of chapter 6, which is a primer on the HOLC. We hope this will serve as a valuable reference for anyone interested in learning the basic aspects of how the HOLC operated.

The third part of the book analyzes the HOLC as an economic intervention. Chapter 7 details Rose's work about how the HOLC interacted with lenders. Chapter 8 considers borrowers. That chapter, along with the story of Joshua Clark told in the introduction, describes what it was like to be a home owner with a mortgage loan during the Great Depression, and gives a clear picture of how Americans benefited from assistance by the HOLC. Joshua's lender said, "We are not willing to carry him." That summarizes the era better than any other words we can muster. Chapter 9 synthesizes the work of the two research teams regarding how the HOLC affected mortgage and housing markets over the decade of the 1930s.

The analysis closes in chapter 10 by providing a detailed accounting of the costs of the HOLC to the US Treasury and the nation's taxpayers. We debunk the popular conception that the HOLC made a profit. Instead, it was likely the source of a small loss to taxpayers, a loss that should be weighed against the benefits it provided to borrowers, lenders, and mortgage and housing markets.

In the book's conclusion, we discuss what we have learned about the HOLC, and relate the book to the recent mortgage crisis and efforts that have been made to mitigate it. Crises of these sorts are rare events. Each therefore deserves study on its own and for the sake of comparison. The value of history here is not to uncover exact parallels to current events, however, but to clarify how the incentives and behavior of borrowers, lenders, and other economic actors during crises transcend vastly different institutional contexts to shape the impacts and effectiveness of policy. Along the way, the Depression provides us with a still powerful reminder of how things could go so wrong, and the HOLC provides an important alternative view of how policy can address such a crisis.

In writing this book, we have benefited from the support and insights of many colleagues. First and foremost are our co-authors. The research underlying this book benefited tremendously from Snowden's collaboration with Charles Courtemanche and Fishback's collaboration with Alfonso Flores-Lagunes, William Horrace, Shawn Kantor, and Jaret Treber. We thank several people for valuable insights after reading early versions of the manuscript, including Claudia Goldin, Joe Elling, two anonymous referees, students in Fishback's graduate economic history class at the University of Arizona, and Alison and James Rose.

A note on a convention we use throughout the text. Many details from the case files of individual HOLC borrowers are available from documents at the National Archives. We changed the names of any borrowers whose information is taken from these files. For those interested in conducting further research, the citations still lead to the boxes at the archives.

For acknowledgments, sources of research support, and disclosure of the author's material financial relationships, if any, please see www.nber.org/chapters/c12909.ack.

Finally, a disclaimer: the views expressed here are solely the responsibility of the authors and should not be interpreted as reflecting the views of the Board of Governors of the Federal Reserve System or of anyone else associated with the Federal Reserve System.

# Acknowledgments

Price Fishback is deeply indebted to Shawn Kantor, Alfonso Flores-Lagunes, William Horrace, and Jaret Treber for their help as coauthors on some of the work described in the book. They—along with Larry Neal, Joseph Mason, Michael Haines, John Wallis, and Trevor Kollman—provided a great deal of help in obtaining the data used in the book. I have also benefited from the comments of Charles Courtemanche, Daniel Fetter, Claudia Goldin, Gary Gorton, Chris Hanes, Kei Hirano, Joe Jackson, Harry Kelejian, Robert Margo, Kris Mitchener, David Pervin, Jonathan Rose, David Wheelock, Eugene White, and workshop participants at the University of California, Davis, the University of Kentucky, the University of Maryland, the University of Nevada, Las Vegas, the University of North Carolina, Oxford, Royal Holloway, and Yale, as well as participants at the 2001 and 2008 NBER Summer Institutes and 2001 Economic History Association meetings. Financial support has been provided by National Science Foundation Grants SBR-9708098, SES-0080324, SES-0214483, SES-0617972, SES-0921732, and SES-1061927, the Earhart Foundation, the University of Arizona Foundation, the University of Arizona Office of the Vice President for Research, the Frank and Clara Kramer Professorship in Economics at the University of Arizona, and the Thomas R. Brown Professorship at Arizona. My mother, Fran Fishback, and sister, Taylor Deibel, taught me how to enjoy life while working hard to be a productive member of society. I owe the largest debt to my wife, Pam Slaten, who has been the love of my life while supporting me in all of my work, even while I tended to spend too much time in working on my research.

Kenneth Snowden acknowledges Charles Courtemanche, Price Fishback, and Jonathan Rose for their collegiality, guidance, and unlimited assistance in all elements of this project. He is also indebted to Charles Calomiris, Naomi Lamoreaux, Richard Sylla, David Wheelock, and Eugene White for insights that have shaped my understanding of the historical mortgage markets in which the HOLC operated. The analysis presented here benefited from the comments of participants at workshops at the Federal Reserve Bank of St. Louis, Rutgers, Yale, UCLA, and UNC Greensboro; at the EHA Session at the 2010 ASSA; and the 2010 spring meeting of the NBER's Development of American Economy program. Financial support has been provided by National Science Foundation Grant SES-1061927. I thank Dyan Arkin for all the rest that matters.

Jonathan Rose thanks Price Fishback and Kenneth Snowden for sharing their knowledge and wisdom. The analysis presented here benefited from the comments of workshop participants at the University of California, Berkeley, the Federal Reserve Board, the St. Louis Federal Reserve Bank, and the All UC Group in Economic History, particularly those of Barry Eichengreen, Chris Hanes, Kris Mitchener, Martha Olney, Christina and David Romer, David Wheelock, and Eugene White. Large parts of this research would not have been possible without the generous acts of Claudia Goldin and the staff at the NBER in tracking down the microfilmed records of HOLC loans. I owe the largest debt to my family for their love and support.

# CHAPTER 1

## INTRODUCTION

---

Joshua Clark nearly lost his house. It was a typical bungalow in Coeur d'Alene, Idaho, with six rooms, one bath, and a cedar-shake roof, home to Joshua, his wife, Sarah, and their teenage son. The family had saved enough from Joshua's work as a truck driver for Inland Motor Freight to put down $1,750 in cash for the house that they bought for $3,000 in March 1929, near the end of the 1920s boom. They borrowed the rest from the Citizens Savings and Loan Society in nearby Spokane, Washington. Putting down 50 percent or more of the value of the house was routine at the time. It ensured borrowers had much to lose if they stopped making payments on their houses, and with limited competition among lenders, borrowers had few options.[1]

Sadly, Sarah soon fell ill and died in the early 1930s. As her health deteriorated, the doctor bills mounted. When Sarah died, Joshua still owed on his mortgage loan and medical debts. In other economic times, he might have been able to find a way to repay the debts through hard work and thrift. The early 1930s was not such a period. Like many Americans, Joshua couldn't get out of debt. Throughout the 1920s he had been making $2,000 a year or more. In 1933 his income was only about $1,200, and that was better than in 1931 and 1932. He tried to work overtime, but with nearly 20 percent of Idaho workers having lost their jobs in the first two years of the Great Depression, such overtime work was not easy to come by. He could sell his house and rent, but because there were few buyers and housing prices had dropped, that would not have solved the problem.[2]

In October 1931 Joshua stopped making mortgage loan payments. At some point, Citizens began to warn of foreclosure. The city and county governments also likely began pressing him to take care of $290 in property taxes, unpaid after 1930. But neither the local government nor Citizens moved quickly to foreclose. Instead, Joshua stayed in his home for two and a half years after stopping payments and before applying to the Home Owners' Loan Corporation (HOLC) in May 1934. The HOLC had been created one year earlier during the first days of the Roosevelt administration, to help mortgage borrowers like Joshua hold on to their homes and work their way out of debt. Citizens may have stalled because the housing market was in grave decline in 1931 and 1932. In such an environment, Citizens would have been stuck with a house it could not easily sell. Furthermore, with no one living there and maintaining the house, it would have lost value. Citizens sought to protect its investment. If the economy improved, Joshua might begin to repay, and if he could not, then foreclosure could be reconsidered in a stronger market. After all, Citizens would not have expected the Great Depression to last as long or become as severe as it did.

By mid-1934, however, Joshua's mortgage was an investment that the bank probably wished it did not have, but could not easily get rid of. In 1933 Idaho adopted a mortgage moratorium law that legally delayed foreclosures. Of the forty-eight states at the time, twenty-seven passed moratoria as a way to pause the system in the midst of a torrent of foreclosures. Idaho also adopted a law that would have limited Citizens' ability to get a court order, called a deficiency judgment, under which Joshua would have been liable for the balance of his loan if the sale of his property was not enough to clear his debt. By 1934, Citizens simply stated, "We are not willing to carry him." This was a decision that many lenders eventually reached by 1933 or 1934, and they directed their borrowers to find financing elsewhere or face foreclosure.[3]

Both Joshua's inability to pay and Citizens' unwillingness to carry him were common. By 1933 foreclosures were widespread across the country, as lender forbearance did not last indefinitely. Just a few years earlier in the 1920s, the situation had been quite different. Both lenders and borrowers expected property values at least to stay stable and in many areas to rise. Lenders took comfort in relatively conservative lending standards. By requiring large down payments, lenders had wide margins of safety in case of foreclosure. Foreclosures had been limited in the nonfarm sector during the 1920s. When they did happen, the lenders were accustomed to quickly recouping their losses by selling into a strong market. Lenders were well compensated for these risks with interest rates that were fairly high by modern standards. But it is the rare mortgage loan system that is built to deal with credit problems on the scale of those generated by the Great Depression. As nonfarm foreclosures piled up between 1926 and 1933, it became clear that the 1920s mortgage loan system was not up to the task. Foreclosures reached all parts of the country. As a sign of the times, after four years of depression, in the spring of 1933 a thousand New Yorkers met at church every Monday night, to pray for those facing foreclosure.[4]

Enter the HOLC, a federally owned corporation created in June 1933. The HOLC was charged with buying the mortgage loans of home owners "in hard straits largely through no fault of their own" from lenders like Citizens, and then refinancing them on more generous terms. The HOLC itself adopted the "no fault of their own" frame to emphasize that the origins of the mortgage crisis lay largely in the general economic collapse. Joshua must have felt that the characterization fit him when he applied to the HOLC for refinancing in May 1934 after two and half years of not paying his mortgage. The HOLC had his house appraised and found the value had fallen nearly 20 percent, from $3,000 in 1929 to $2,500 in 1934. Citizens and Joshua were in better shape than many, because average housing prices had fallen roughly 35 percent or more in many parts of the country. After several months of evaluating the loan and negotiating with Citizens, the HOLC purchased the loan in February 1935.[5]

The HOLC treated this like most of its cases. Using HOLC bonds, the agency purchased Joshua's loan from Citizens for the full value of the debt that Joshua still owed Citizens. Citizens received a good deal. It got rid of a "toxic" loan—on which it had received at best sporadic payments for two to three years—in exchange for HOLC bonds, which were equal in value to the full amount of the various debts that Joshua owed the lender. Citizens even received the lost interest that Joshua had not paid, and did not have to deal with the costs of foreclosing on a home and then trying to repair and sell it in a market in which almost nothing sold. On its books, Citizens jettisoned a toxic asset with low expected value and replaced it with a no-risk asset of much higher value.

Once the HOLC owned Joshua's original loan, they replaced it with a new one that better reflected his situation. The principal on the HOLC loan consolidated his various debts, including all the principal and interest he owed his old lender, unpaid taxes, and the cost of repairs ordered by the HOLC. The repairs included new shingles on the roof and new paint for the outside woodwork. The rest of the loan terms were generous. The interest rate was 5 percent, when even borrowers who were in good shape in the Mountain West faced rates of 8 percent in the private market. The rate was particularly low given that Joshua hadn't been paying his mortgage loan and property taxes for more than two years. No regular lender would have made him a loan at *any* interest rate. The payments on the HOLC loan were spread evenly over fifteen years in an amortized arrangement, so that there was no big balloon payment at the end. Instead of trying to pay an immediate bill of roughly $300 in property taxes and losing his home when the Idaho mortgage moratorium ended, Joshua now had a newly repaired home and a low monthly payment.

There are more than a million stories like Joshua's to be found among the people whose loans were bought and refinanced by the HOLC between 1933 and 1936. Ray was a researcher at a large department store in Chicago for twenty years but lost his job and found his gray hair to be a barrier to reemployment. He was considering moving in with his daughter and son-in-law. Lee, a real estate broker in Detroit, was living in his foreclosed house as a tenant because his lender was not legally able to sell it until 1935. His mother helped him out with the rent. Antonio, a stonemason in Princeton, New Jersey, and Edwin, a dance instructor in Detroit, each lost their steady stream of customers as the economy nose-dived. These were all people whom the HOLC deemed in danger of losing their homes "through no fault of their own."[6]

In just three years the HOLC refinanced loans for a million borrowers like Joshua, Ray, Lee, Antonio, and Edwin. By 1936, 10 percent of American nonfarm home owners were HOLC borrowers. Nearly as many applied to the HOLC and were turned down. For some of those failed applications, HOLC negotiations with the lenders broke down, while for others the HOLC determined the borrowers had enough resources to repay their loans without aid. The large scale of the HOLC's operation shows just how much havoc the foreclosure crisis wreaked throughout the nation during the Great Depression. This book explains how the HOLC worked and the impact it had on borrowers, lenders, local housing markets, and taxpayers.

### The HOLC as a Response to a Mortgage Crisis
### Following the 1920s Boom

The New Deal created many programs that attempted to cope with the economic depression, addressing unemployment rates that exceeded 20 percent for several years, disastrous drops in farm incomes, and myriad other problems not rooted in the housing sector. The HOLC was specifically designed to address the crisis in nonfarm housing and needs to be understood within the context of the housing market and mortgage finance system in which it operated.

A residential construction boom in the 1920s accompanied a wave of innovations that transformed the residential mortgage loan industry. The boom had begun to slow by the late 1920s, and the Great Depression turned a softening housing market into a deeply troubled one that involved hundreds of thousands of foreclosures in the first half of the 1930s.

The expansion of mortgage debt during the 1920s involved the use of a variety of contracts, including short-term loans with balloon payments at the end, longer-term contracts offered by building and loan associations (B&Ls) with uniquely structured monthly payments, and a rapid expansion of junior mortgages. Each of these was fundamentally different than the typical modern mortgage loan contract. The older contracts seemed to work well in the 1920s but turned out to be quite vulnerable to the shocks in income and housing prices that took the country by surprise during the Depression.

By the time the HOLC was created in the spring of 1933, the mortgage crisis had been gathering force for nearly three years, and the mortgage and housing markets were in free fall. In 1931 President Hoover and a Republican Congress tried to deal with the problem by developing the Federal Home Loan Bank system, which was designed to provide more funds for lenders facing short-term problems. States also tried to stem the tide by enacting foreclosure moratoria beginning in early 1933. Neither was able to turn the tide of foreclosures. By 1933 a coalition of borrowers, lenders, and real estate professionals throughout the United States sought immediate and dramatic action at the federal level.

During Roosevelt's first hundred days in office, the HOLC was created to buy troubled mortgages from lenders and refinance them. The goal was to stop house-price declines by delaying foreclosure and modifying the terms of payment so that borrowers had more time to find jobs and generate income flows once the economy improved. A critical element in evaluating this program, therefore, is to assess its underlying rationale that the private mortgage market in 1933 could not resolve the mortgage crisis it had created. Although individual lenders recognized the costs imposed on the economy by the foreclosure crisis, such as empty homes and downward pressure on house prices, no individual lender could alter the crisis on its own, and therefore had little incentive to take these costs into account when choosing between foreclosure and modification of a loan.

Collective action in the form of a large-scale modification program like the HOLC was proposed as a solution and was supported by a variety of groups including borrowers, lenders, and real estate professionals. But collective action by the private sector was limited at best. By 1933 private lenders had not successfully developed anything remotely like a large-scale "bad bank" to deal with the foreclosure crisis. There were many types of lenders facing different types of regulations and incentives. More fundamentally, financing for such a venture likely would have been difficult. If private bad banks had issued bonds to the public in order to fund such an operation, they would have had to pay high interest rates, which in turn would have required them to charge higher interest rates to borrowers, reflecting the risks inherent in those troubled loans. In turn, higher interest rates would have increased the probability that borrowers would default on the loans, creating even more risk. In contrast, the federal government guaranteed the HOLC bonds, allowing the HOLC to obtain funding at a much lower cost and to offer low interest rates to borrowers.

## Then and Now

Modern readers will evaluate the HOLC with fresh perspective, created by their own experiences, which likely are heavily shaped by the mortgage crisis of the early 2000s. The housing boom of the 1920s and bust of the 1930s rival the huge rise and fall in housing markets during the first decade of the 2000s, but the mechanisms underlying the parallel events were not always the same. Loans were more conservatively underwritten in the 1920s, creating a margin of safety, but nevertheless the nonfarm mortgage finance system was far more fragile in 1930 than in 2007. In the 1930s, Fannie Mae and Freddie Mac were not around to purchase loans and keep the credit flowing, so new loans disappeared from 1932 to 1934 to an extent without parallel. Because of this the

HOLC was able to play a unique role in providing credit to those like Joshua, whose lender was "not willing to carry him." At the same time, the conservative underwriting standards of the 1920s left the HOLC room to maneuver when modifying the loans it purchased.

The structure of the HOLC also differed in important ways from the interventions of the years after 2007. Most importantly, the HOLC both bought and refinanced troubled mortgages, while recent policy has worked to prevent foreclosures without purchasing the loans from the lenders. As a result, the HOLC owned the loans for the long term, had the ability to control how the loans were serviced, and had a strong incentive to use that ability to make continued efforts to avoid foreclosures. These efforts were matched by the actions of Congress, which liberalized HOLC loan terms even further in 1939 to avoid widespread defaults among HOLC borrowers.

## What We Have Learned

Throughout the book, we show how the HOLC affected the housing finance market and the broader economy during the 1930s. Ultimately, the HOLC's impact can be summarized in four broad statements.

First, the HOLC served as a "bad bank" by buying "toxic assets" from lenders. The HOLC could not force lenders to participate: the only way it could succeed at buying a large number of loans was by offering lenders a good deal. It usually paid prices that were nearly as large as the full debts owed to lenders. In this way the HOLC addressed the problem of toxic assets that modern policy has struggled with since the financial meltdown in 2008. The goal was not just to bail out everybody in the market, though. Instead, the agency was selective in its purchase of loans. They focused on the loans of home owners in trouble "through no fault of their own" and who were likely to repay their loans once they had survived the hard times and reached firmer footing.

Second, the HOLC succeeded in reaching a large number of distressed home owners—about one in five of all nonfarm mortgage borrowers—by refinancing their mortgages on generous terms even though its ability to deliver debt reductions was limited. The HOLC's goal was not simply to bail out borrowers but also to keep people who were likely to repay in their homes until the hard times were over. To this end, the agency wrote loans large enough so that borrowers could pay off tax debts and, if necessary, repair their homes. The HOLC provided these loans at below-market interest rates to borrowers who had no real chance of getting refinancing anywhere else. Until June 1936—the first three years of the HOLC's operations—borrowers had the option of paying interest only and then settling into the normal features of the new loan. The loans were amortized into equal monthly payments, so no large payment loomed at the end of the loan, and the repayment schedule was spread over fifteen years. Although long-term amortized loans were offered in some corners of the housing finance market before 1930, in just a few short years the HOLC gave its borrowers access to these loans, part of a wholesale change in lending practices across the country.

Third, the HOLC reduced the damage caused by the foreclosure crisis of the 1930s, but it did not reverse all of its impacts. Most directly, the HOLC ended up foreclosing on 20 percent of its borrowers. In the broader market, the HOLC did not fully resolve home owners' problems, as the nationwide foreclosure rate continued at high levels through 1937. Overall, housing prices and home ownership declined in the 1930s, but they would have declined still further without the HOLC. We have not been able to measure the impact of the HOLC on the largest housing markets with much confidence, but our research shows that HOLC activity in many communities had large, positive impacts on maintaining housing values and home-ownership rates. In a typical small community, HOLC lending staved off about a 16 percent decline in the value of homes and kept about 11 percent more home owners in their homes.

Finally, by the time the HOLC dissolved itself in 1951, it lost a total of about $53 million, or roughly 2 percent of its total lending volume of around $3 billion. Recent discussions of the HOLC have mistakenly emphasized that it actually made money and thus did not impose costs on taxpayers, but our careful examination suggests that this perception is mistaken. In addition, there was an implicit subsidy to housing markets because the federal government guaranteed the HOLC bonds and thus allowed the corporation to issue them at lower interest rates. Had the HOLC needed to pay an extra 1 percent in interest on the bonds it issued, the cost of the program to the taxpayer would have risen from about 2 percent to about 12 percent. The HOLC was not free, but neither did it cost taxpayers much money in the grand scheme of the federal budget. At a relatively low cost, the HOLC was able to prevent a substantial number of foreclosures and significant loss of home value.

# CHAPTER 2

# THE PATCHWORK
# MORTGAGE MARKET
# IN THE 1920S

---

Home building added more than its fair share to the roar of the 1920s. A residential construction boom was fueled by rapid income growth and population expansion in urban areas, particularly in the South and West.[1] These new homes were funded by a historic expansion of residential mortgage debt through a diverse set of lenders using a variety of contracts. The boom led to peaks in nonfarm home ownership and mortgage debt.

Yet the boom did not obviously contribute to the subsequent mortgage crisis in the same way that the housing boom of the early 2000s did to the recent crisis. Although the volume of mortgage lending expanded to meet the intense demand during the 1920s, the structure of the contracts that were used ultimately proved to increase the fragility of the mortgage market more than any deterioration in lending standards. For this reason these loan practices generally disappeared during the crisis of the 1930s. In this chapter we describe the patchwork mortgage market of the 1920s and why it ultimately failed during the Depression. When the HOLC was created in 1933, it was created with the background of a generation of new borrowers and lenders who discovered that, after four years of devastating depression, their home investments were far more vulnerable than they could ever have anticipated.

## The 1920s Boom

The United States entered the 1920s facing an acute demand for more housing that had appeared during World War I. The housing shortage was quickly

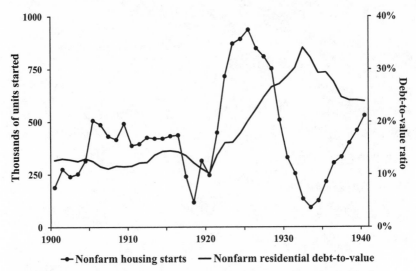

**Figure 2.1.** *Nonfarm residential housing starts and debt-to-value ratios for the United States, 1900–1940. (Data from Grebler, Blank, and Winnick 1956, table L.6.)*

relieved, however, by an unprecedented home-building boom. The volume of residential construction during the 1920s (figure 2.1) rose out of all proportion relative to earlier production levels and more than offset the impact of wartime dislocation. Annual nonfarm housing production during the 1920s nearly doubled its 1900–1910 level and sustained levels between 1922 and 1928 more than 50 percent higher than the peak in any previous year.[2] The volume of nonfarm mortgage debt that financed nonfarm residential construction rose even more rapidly than the rise in the nonfarm housing stock during the decade. As a result, the ratio of residential mortgage debt to residential housing wealth more than doubled, from 14 percent to nearly 30 percent in the 1920s.[3]

Although the growth rate of home mortgage lending was faster during the 1920s than in any other period of similar length in the twentieth century, the expansion took place within a market that was still financially immature relative to modern standards. Mortgages were not used nearly so widely in 1920 as they are today. Only 41 percent of the nation's nonfarm housing units were owner-occupied in that year, and only 40 percent of those properties were mortgaged.[4] Individuals and other non-institutional investors held more than 40 percent of outstanding residential mortgage debt, compared to virtually none today, as shown in figure 2.2.[5] Borrowers seeking second mortgages most often dealt with these non-institutional lenders. Further, the federal government played a very limited role in the 1920s markets. The only federally supervised mortgage lenders were national banks, and for most of the decade federal regulations prohibited them from holding more than a small portion of their assets in residential mortgage debt. The result was a patchwork of largely local mortgage finance institutions with fragmented regulation and supervision by state governments.

During the 1920s, mortgage lending through mutual savings banks, commercial banks, and life insurance companies grew nearly as fast as the overall market, but there were important limitations on the lending activities of each of these groups. Mutual savings banks were heavily concentrated in New

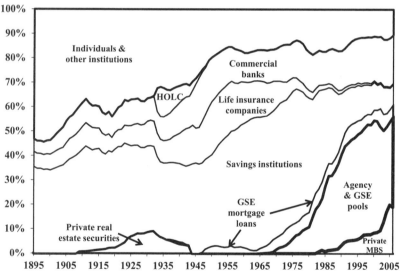

**Figure 2.2.** *Sources of nonfarm residential mortgage debt, 1896–2007. Savings institutions include mutual savings banks, B&Ls, and savings and loans. GSE stands for government-supported enterprises, such as Fannie Mae and Freddie Mac, and MBS stands for mortgage-backed security. (Data for 1896–1944 from Grebler, Blank, and Winnick 1956, tables N.1, N.2. Data for 1945–2008 from Board of Governors of the Federal Reserve System, Z-1 statistical release.)*

England and the mid-Atlantic region but virtually absent in the South and West, where state-chartered commercial banks and affiliated mortgage companies and brokers often served as significant lenders. Eastern life insurance companies, on the other hand, had been the largest interregional farm mortgage lenders for decades but had just started to expand into the residential field in the 1920s.

The fastest-growing and most active institutional mortgage lenders were the B&Ls. The typical B&L was a small, local institution owned mutually by members who contributed weekly or monthly dues that were pooled and lent to other members as home mortgages. By 1920 B&Ls were operating in every state. B&Ls were typically not constrained by the entry barriers facing most regulated financial institutions, because people seeking to organize new charters rarely needed to demonstrate to regulators that local credit needs were not being met by existing institutions. As a result, the number of B&Ls grew from eight thousand to thirteen thousand during the 1920s, B&L membership rose from four to twelve million people, and total assets rose from $2.5 billion to $8 billion. B&Ls also responded more aggressively than other lenders to the regional shift of population and home building to southern and western markets.[6]

## Mortgage Contracts

A variety of different mortgage loan types were used in the residential mortgage market during the 1920s lending boom. None matched the thirty-year, amortized, fixed-rate mortgage that has dominated lending since World War II. The modern amortized loan contract specifies equal monthly payments with no balloon payment at the end, although amortization has a more general meaning of paying off debt over time with regular payments. Short-term balloon mortgages had long been the most common contract form, but the expansion of B&Ls led to a large number of borrowers with B&L-style contracts known as share-accumulation contracts, explained further below. To borrow more than 50 or 60 percent of the value of the home, borrowers had to take out second mortgages at much higher interest rates from nontraditional lenders. In the Chicago and New York metropolitan areas, mortgage guarantee companies followed the modern practice of developing bonds backed by mortgages. However, the bonds accounted for a relatively small share of mortgage funding, in contrast to the active market in mortgage-backed securities that developed at the turn of the twenty-first century. Each of the mortgage contracts contained specific design elements that were not problematic in normal periods but helped transmit and amplify the foreclosure crisis that developed in the 1930s.

## SHORT-TERM BALLOON LOANS

Short-term balloon loans were among the most common mortgages in use before 1930. They usually lasted for a short time, such as from three to five years, were written for no more than 60 percent of the property value, and required only interest payments during the life of the contract. At the end of the loan, a borrower repaid the principal in what is known as a "balloon payment" because the principal was typically more than one hundred times larger than the monthly payment. For example, under a five-year contract for a loan of $1,000 at 6 percent interest, a borrower paid $5 in interest to the lender each month for five years. At the end of the five-year period, the borrower then repaid the $1,000 of principal.

These contracts had been used for decades in the farm and commercial mortgage markets in the United States, even though borrowers often complained bitterly about the short term of these loans relative to the long-term investments in land they were used to finance. The mismatch meant that borrowers normally had to renew or "roll over" the loan one or more times before they could afford to save enough to repay the entire principal. These renewals, borrowers alleged, opened them to risks regarding changes in interest rates, additional commission charges, changes in underwriting standards, and excessive legal fees. Farmers' complaints about these mortgage contracts intensified in the decade before World War I. In 1916 the US Congress established the Federal Farm Loan System, which began offering farmers relatively long-term, amortized mortgages with equal payments throughout the loan term. No parallel system was set up for nonfarm residential loans, however.

Many lenders relied on these traditional renewable, short-term balloon loans during the 1920s. Mutual savings banks, for example, were some of the oldest mortgage-lending institutions in the nation and were heavily concentrated in large urban markets in New England and the mid-Atlantic states. A study of residential mortgage loans made by Massachusetts mutual savings banks between 1918 and 1931 found that only one-tenth of nearly ten thousand loans used amortization to even out the payments and reduce the size of the balloon payment at the end of the loan. Even then, the scheduled principal payments on the few loans that did use amortization were often unpaid.[7]

Commercial banks were most active as mortgage lenders in the South and West and were often required by regulation to hold only short-term loans. Mutual savings banks faced similar requirements. Two out of three loans in a national sample of home mortgages made by commercial banks during the 1920s were written for terms of four years or less. Eastern life insurance companies also served western and southern markets through interregional lending networks that they had developed over decades of activity as important farm mortgage lenders. Although the insurance companies relied heavily on straight mortgage loans during the 1920s, they offered longer repayment schedules and made more use of partial amortization than did savings and commercial banks. Individual investors, who held two-fifths of the residential mortgage debt in the 1920s, probably relied even more heavily on short-term balloon loans than these institutional lenders, because long-term amortized loans carried more lending risks and expenses.[8]

## BUILDING AND LOAN SHARE-ACCUMULATION CONTRACTS

B&Ls were the most important institutional residential mortgage lenders in the 1920s. B&Ls relied most heavily on a "share-accumulation" mortgage contract that provided the borrower with the ability to make monthly payments that slowly added up, so that the principal debt could be repaid without a large payment at the end of the contract. This method was similar to amortization, but the difference lay in how the monthly payments were applied. An amortizing mortgage contract applies the non-interest portion of a monthly payment directly to reducing the principal debt at the time the payment is made. As a result, the amount of principal to be repaid is reduced each time a payment is made. In contrast, the B&L share-accumulation contract invested the non-interest portion of the monthly payment in the shares of the B&L association. Those shares constituted a "sinking fund." Over time the payments into the sinking fund earned dividends and accumulated to the point at which the funds equaled the principal on the loan. At that time the sinking fund was then used to pay the principal of the loan in full, and the borrower received full title to his home. As a result, the borrower owed the entire principal throughout the period of the loan. If the sinking fund assets fell in value, the borrower would have to make additional payments until the assets in the sinking fund reached the amount of the principal.

Besides the simulation of amortization, there were several important advantages to the B&L loan contract. First, associations were truly mutual societies because both borrowing and nonborrowing members held full ownership stakes. The mutuality provided both types of members with higher returns on savings than they could obtain on savings accounts at commercial banks. After 1914 members received additional benefits because they did not have to pay federal income tax on deposit accounts, although this advantage accrued to only the small share of households that earned enough income to be required to pay income taxes. Finally, because the share-accumulation contract created a sinking fund, the incentive for the borrowing member to repay became stronger throughout the life of the loan. Failure to make payments and defaults on the loan meant that members lost not only the house but also the accumulated value in the sinking fund. In contrast, balloon loans gave no such incentive. With this additional security, B&Ls were able to offer borrowers not only longer maturities than other lenders but also larger loan amounts that ran up to 60 percent or even two-thirds of the property's value.[9]

## THE PROLIFERATION OF SECOND MORTGAGE LOANS

The 50 to 60 percent loan-to-value ratio requirement for first mortgage loans kept many potential home owners of good character from purchasing homes because they had not yet saved enough for a down payment. As lenders and borrowers looked for methods to relax the high down-payment requirements, the use of second mortgage loans proliferated in the 1920s. H. Morton Bodfish, one of the leading chroniclers of housing markets at the time, provided a snapshot of how extensively second mortgages were used in Chicago. He collected public records on the original financing of sixty-nine homes purchased over a three-month period in 1925. One-half of the transfers were financed with only first mortgages with an average loan-to-value ratio of about 50 percent. The remaining loans were financed with both first and second mortgages and had average loan-to-value ratios of 64 percent; the ratios were 41 percent on the first mortgage and 23 percent on the second. For both groups, on average, the first mortgage loans had five-year maturities, interest rates of 6 percent, and commissions and fees that added 1.2 percent to the annual effective interest rate. The second loans, on the other hand, carried much higher effective interest rates of 11.6 percent with an added requirement that each borrower pay 2 percent of the second loan principal every month so that it would be fully repaid over just five years. There were substantial costs, therefore, associated with the use of second mortgage financing.[10]

A 1931 investigation also shows how deeply second mortgage loans had become embedded in the mortgage market by the end of the 1920s. A survey of lenders in West Coast cities indicated that two-thirds to three-quarters of borrowers used first and second mortgages. The average loan-to-value ratio for homes that combined the two ranged between 70 and 75 percent. As in Chicago, interest rates on second mortgage loans were substantially higher than on first mortgage loans. Second mortgage lenders held junior liens on the home, which meant that in a foreclosure, the first mortgage lender received full compensation before the second mortgage lender received any payments. The greater risk from the junior lien contributed to the higher interest rate on the second mortgage loan.[11]

The investigation also reported that the second mortgage loan market was institutionally immature. Most of these loans were made by the previous owner for existing homes and by home builders and building-material suppliers for newly constructed homes—the large set of non-institutional investors in figure 2.2. Relatively few financial firms specialized in second mortgages, even in the largest urban centers.

## MORTGAGE GUARANTEES AND EARLY MORTGAGE-BACKED SECURITIES

Mortgage guarantee companies brought two innovations to the residential mortgage market in the 1920s—private mortgage insurance and the creation of a form of mortgage-backed securities. At first the companies offered mortgage insurance as a stand-alone product, but in the 1910s some guarantee companies began to combine it with mortgage banking by originating, selling, and servicing loans that they had insured. In 1921 only twelve companies in New York were active in this business, but by 1930 some fifty guarantee companies in the state had written insurance on $3 billion in loans, equal to one-tenth of all outstanding residential mortgage debt, on mortgages that they had originated and marketed.

The guarantee companies helped develop a secondary market for loans by selling them to investors. They sold about $2 billion in insured loans as whole loans to investors. When marketing the remaining $1 billion in insured loans, they also created two types of mortgage-backed securities by placing mortgages in trust accounts against which the companies issued "collateral trust certificates of participation." Some of the trusts contained only a single insured mortgage, and certificates were issued to several investors. Other trusts contained pools of insured mortgages, and "group certificates" were issued in a manner similar to modern mortgage-backed securities.[12]

## The Beginnings of a Decline

By 1929 the forces that had been driving the housing and mortgage boom of the 1920s had about played out. The peak of the housing production boom had occurred in 1925, although housing starts continued to exceed prewar levels. The ratio of mortgage debt to home values, on the other hand, continued to climb into the early 1930s to levels never seen before. Part of the reason for the rise was the decline in housing values that began sometime between 1925 and 1930. Nonetheless, there was little concern expressed at the time that mortgage indebtedness represented a danger. By modern standards the debt-to-value ratios, known as "leverage," were not excessive, even in hindsight. The mortgage lending contracts seemed to be working reasonably well despite the declines in housing prices and building activity in the late 1920s.

But each of the mortgage contracts in the 1920s turned out to be much more fragile to the shocks associated with the Great Depression than borrowers or lenders could have imagined a few years before. The short-term balloon loan was so common during the 1920s that millions of home owners were stuck trying to renew their mortgages in the early 1930s just as the Great Depression and the foreclosure crisis began to accelerate. Many lenders came under pressure at the same time. Households were drawing down savings and thus withdrawing deposits and cashing out life insurance policies, while lenders' investments were failing. As a result, funds available for loans declined sharply.

When balloon payments came due, a number of lenders allowed borrowers to continue making interest payments in hopes that the borrowers could regain footing and repay the principal. Even in cases where lenders were willing to renew, borrowers found it increasingly difficult to pay the fixed administrative costs of the renewal process because of reductions in work hours or job loss. The problem was exacerbated further as home values fell and borrowers had to come up with extra funds to ensure that the loan-to-value ratio on the loan stayed below 60 percent.

If a borrower could find a lender willing to roll over the loan or temporarily allow a continuation of the loan at the same nominal interest rate, the situation was still dire. The annual average 6.7 percent rate of deflation between

1929 and 1933 meant that each dollar repaid was more valuable than the dollar the home owner originally borrowed. Irving Fisher, an economist widely renowned for his work on interest rates, provided the basic framework that is still used today for thinking about these issues. Fisher defined the "real" rate of interest as the interest rate after adjusting for the percentage changes in the price level. In his simplest calculations, the real rate was defined as the "nominal" interest rate on a loan contract minus the growth rate of the price level. In the late 1920s, when interest rates on mortgage loans averaged around 6 percent and the price level grew 1 percent, the real rate of interest was around 5 percent. In the 1930s the nominal rate on mortgage loans stayed around 6 percent, but the deflation of 6.7 percent meant that the price level was growing at −6.7 percent. After subtracting the −6.7 percent inflation rate from the 6 percent nominal rate, the real rate of interest had grown to 12.7 percent. This real rate of interest was roughly double the level of the highest real mortgage loan rate the United States has seen since, and quadruple the typical real rate over the century before this book was written. The problems of renewing the mortgage loans combined with the extraordinarily high real costs of loans placed home mortgage borrowers at greater risk of default and foreclosure as the economy sank deeper into the Great Depression.[13]

Some lenders, like Citizens Savings and Loan Society in dealing with Joshua in chapter 1, waited to foreclose even though borrowers were making no payments. After some time, however, lenders chose to foreclose, often because they faced their own liabilities to depositors, shareholders, or the insured. Too large a share of unpaid mortgages on a lender's books could lead to the failure of the lender.

There was also an important weakness in the share-accumulation mortgage loan contract that eventually caused severe distress among thousands of B&Ls and their members when the housing crisis expanded. Borrowing and nonborrowing members in a B&L shared in the association's losses as well as its profits. Sharing of profits during the 1920s was quite popular, as it meant that sinking funds accumulated at even faster paces. But when profits turned to losses, sinking funds shrank. During the mortgage crisis of the 1930s, many borrowers in B&Ls saw their share accounts decrease in value as other members in their association defaulted on their own payments on the mortgage loans and B&L memberships. The decrease in the accounts meant that the borrowers had to increase the total amount that they paid into their sinking funds before they could fully pay off their debts and take full owner-ship in their homes. In this way the disadvantage of investing principal pay-ments in a sinking fund was exposed. This problem is one reason why modern mortgages are constructed so that principal payments are used to directly pay down the debt immediately. The interplay between borrowing members and losses at B&Ls led to widespread failures within the B&L industry, thousands of protracted and complex B&L liquidations, and the complete abandonment of the share-accumulation contract by World War II. The once quite popular share-accumulation contract is now a historical curiosity.

The proliferation of second mortgages just made the foreclosure crisis worse when borrowers fell behind on their home payments or could not pay the principal when a balloon loan came due. In normal times these situa-tions could often be resolved, but the presence of second mortgages during the Depression greatly complicated the negotiations between borrowers and lenders. Even though the contracts specified the procedures for foreclosure in these cases, often lenders were not anxious to incur the costs and losses of foreclosure. Yet the negotiations for modification were more complicated because two lenders were involved. Guaranteed mortgages and mortgage-backed securities created similar problems because the presence of the under-writing house in these transactions represented a third party in all attempts to deal with delinquent mortgages. The problem was similar, but far less serious in volume, to the problems that have arisen in the modern era with mortgage-backed securities.

These weaknesses in mortgage contracts increased pressures within lend-ing markets that helped amplify the foreclosure crisis that accompanied the Great Depression. Simultaneous declines in income and housing prices dur-ing the early 1930s led a large number of home owners to default on their loan payments and lenders to foreclose on them.

# CHAPTER 3

# THE
# MORTGAGE
# CRISIS

By 1933 a national mortgage crisis was at full boil and showed little sign of cooling off, even as recovery began to take hold in many other parts of the economy. With unemployment at record levels, borrowers struggled to keep current on their debts. House prices had declined by roughly a third on a national basis, and it seemed unlikely that they would rise in the near term. As a result, borrowers had trouble clearing their debts by selling their properties. These were the fundamental factors driving the wave of foreclosures. On top of this, the system of home mortgage finance had largely collapsed, and lending activity in 1933 had nearly halted. Borrowers widely reviled the common loan contracts of the 1920s, but alternatives were not yet widely available. Under great pressure from investors and depositors, increasing numbers of lenders pushed borrowers to pay up or move out.

C. Lowell Harriss, a firsthand witness of the mortgage crisis of the 1930s, wrote the seminal study of the HOLC in 1951. He offers a superb condensation of the factors underlying the crisis:

> In the twenties, as in every period of favorable economic conditions, mortgage debt was entered into by individuals with confidence that the burden could be supported without undue difficulty, and mortgage loans were made by financing agencies with satisfaction over the quality of the investment. . . .
>
> What had generally been regarded as a reasonably sound arrangement by all parties concerned proved to be very weak when a set of interrelated

forces combined to bring on a severe depression after 1929 and to disrupt seriously the structure of home-ownership finance. . . .

The ability of individual borrowers to meet mortgage payments was reduced by large-scale unemployment and by income reductions generally, and also by the necessity of meeting payments on installment sales contract obligations, which had increased sharply in the twenties. . . . These and other factors and conditions were, as is well known, mutually unsettling and self-aggravating.[1]

The mortgage crisis of the 1930s exposed serious fragilities within the US mortgage market. Processes designed to limit risks on individual mortgages had worked well when credit risk was tied to the specific mortgage but not when foreclosures were widespread and interconnected. When the shock of the Great Depression led to large numbers of lenders failing and borrowers facing trouble meeting their payments, the processes for offsetting risks broke down.

The HOLC, created in June 1933, was not the first attempt by legislators to mitigate the 1930s foreclosure crisis. Under President Hoover, the federal government set up a set of regional Federal Home Loan Banks to provide more liquidity and funding to lenders, starting in 1932. In 1933, state governments across the country began passing foreclosure moratoria, pausing the system in hopes that delays would provide time to develop a solution. Neither the moratoria nor the new regional home loan banks were very effective. The continuing foreclosure crisis likely endangered more than a million of the roughly ten million nonfarm home owners in 1933 and promised to generate additional disruption throughout the housing market and the general economy. The HOLC was designed to meet an immediate need for help. More fundamental market reforms were to wait for other New Deal programs.

### The 1930s Foreclosure Crisis

There is no more visible manifestation of the dislocation associated with a mortgage crisis than foreclosure. Figure 3.1 shows the mountain of foreclosures that built up during the early 1930s. It provides an unmistakable picture of the duration and severity of foreclosure problems in the 1930s. Nonfarm foreclosures began to accelerate as construction activity fell off in the late 1920s, but the number jumped to new levels exceeding 200,000 per year for

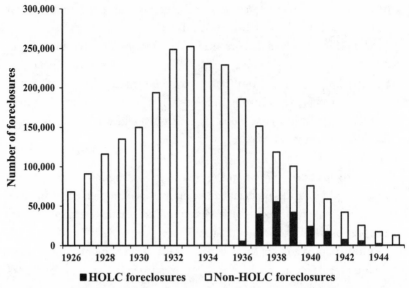

**Figure 3.1.** *Number of foreclosures on nonfarm residential and commercial mortgages in the United States, 1926–1945. (Data from Carter et al. 2006, series DC1255–1270.)*

four full years from 1932 to 1935, before gradually receding over the remainder of the decade.

Ideally, these numbers would allow us to calculate a foreclosure rate, but doing so requires us to make two heroic guesses. First, we need to know the total number of outstanding residential mortgages that were at risk. The 1930 census reported 10.5 million owned nonfarm homes, but unfortunately did not ask about mortgages. A good guess would be about 5.2 million, or 50 percent of owned homes. This guess is a bit higher than the 40 and 46 percent figures reported in the 1920 and 1940 censuses because in 1930 the housing boom had not been undone by very much. A second problem is that the foreclosure data include both residential and commercial properties, making it difficult to calculate a residential mortgage foreclosure rate. We can proceed by inferring from data from a few sources that indicate at least 60 percent of foreclosures in this period were likely on residential properties.[2] With these two bits of information, the foreclosure rate on nonfarm residential mortgages might have been about 2.5–3.0 percent per year at its peak. Over the decade from 1926 to 1936, these data could imply that foreclosure affected 10 to 20 percent of residential mortgages.

In general, the pattern of foreclosures over time has been similar in the 2000s, as the number of residential nonfarm mortgage foreclosures reached a peak in 2009 and has stayed at that high level with the potential for the problems to persist long enough to mirror the 1930s experience. Modern data are much better because they separate out residential properties and the number of mortgaged properties is known. Even with modern data, however, most statistics tabulate the number of foreclosures started or in process, not the number completed. Typically about one-half of foreclosures started end in actual dispossession.[3] During 2010 and 2011, the percentage of loans in the foreclosure process hovered around 4 percent.

In lieu of better foreclosure data, mortgage distress during the 1930s is more accurately measured by a 1934 study of mortgage loan status in twenty-two urban areas. Nearly 45 percent of mortgaged, owner-occupied homes in those areas were delinquent on their payments but had not yet been subject to foreclosure. This rate of delinquency is nearly double the delinquency rates experienced in the most severely affected cities in 2010.[4] However, the delinquency rates in 1934 were likely elevated (and the foreclosure rates depressed) by the presence of mortgage foreclosure moratoria in many states. The mortgage crisis in the 1930s was severe enough that no fewer than twenty-seven of forty-eight states had enacted mortgage foreclosure moratoria, which allowed many home owners to stay in their homes by delaying or suspending foreclosure actions. Additional acts at the state level limited the amounts that borrowers owed to lenders in deficiency judgments, which could be demanded by lenders when foreclosed properties sold for less than the value of the mortgage debts owed.[5]

The foreclosure statistics of 1934, 1935, and 1936 likely would have been much worse in the absence of the HOLC. Between 1933 and 1936, the HOLC refinanced the mortgages of roughly one million home owners who, on average, were more than two years behind on their loan and local property tax payments. Had all of those homes been foreclosed, the number of foreclosures in figure 3.1 for 1934, 1935, and 1936 would have doubled. Even with the HOLC's help, roughly 200,000 borrowers fell behind on the refinanced loan payments hopelessly enough that the HOLC foreclosed. Those HOLC foreclosures are represented by the dark shaded areas at the bottom of each bar after 1935 in figure 3.1.

The ultimate outcome of foreclosure was loss of home ownership, and the vast majority of the households who lost their homes to foreclosure during the 1930s were unable to become home owners again until after 1940, if they ever did. The only decade in which home ownership declined during the twentieth century was the 1930s. The decline from 45.2 percent in 1930 to 41.1 percent in 1940 wiped out most of the 5.2 percentage point rise during the boom of the 1920s. In comparison, home-ownership rates rose from 64.2 percent in 1994 to 69.2 percent in 2004, roughly the same rise as in the 1920s. Since then the rate has fallen by 3.3 percentage points with the potential for further drops to come.[6]

## The Double Trigger

In the modern economics literature, a popular way to understand foreclosures is that they are typically caused by a "double trigger": falling house prices combined with reductions in borrowers' incomes, most often due to unemployment.[7] The double trigger theory suggests that house-price declines by themselves are not generally sufficient to cause foreclosures. This may sound overly optimistic, but the economic reasoning is sound. Suppose a family purchases a $100,000 house, with a down payment of $20,000 and a loan of $80,000. Then the property's value falls to $70,000, leaving them "underwater" because the family owes more on the loan than the value of the house. The family likely would not default on the loan if their breadwinner(s) kept working, since they could still afford the monthly mortgage payment. After all, paying a month's loan payment does not take away the option of defaulting in the future, and the family still needs a place to live. In effect, the family would, each month, compare whether the cost of paying the mortgage is worth the value of living in the house and being able to default at any time in the future. In addition, the act of default itself can be financially and psychologically costly. A default would force the family to find new housing and harm the family's credit rating, making it difficult to purchase a cheaper home, obtain credit cards, and purchase automobiles or other durable goods with credit. Finally, the value of the home might rise again in the future.

The double trigger framework also suggests that foreclosure is unlikely to be caused solely by reductions in a borrower's income. Consider a scenario in which a home owner experiences a reduction in income but the value of the property remains stable. The reduction in income could have happened because of unemployment or adverse life events, such as health crises, death, or divorce. The home owner would not have to default because she could sell the property and repay the debt in full. Moreover, she recovers more of her down payment, avoids a reduction in her credit rating, and avoids the other disruptions and costs associated with foreclosure.

The double trigger framework recognizes the difficulties confronting home owners when either their incomes or property values fall, but emphasizes that, when affected by only one of these shocks, home owners have the option to avoid foreclosure and the incentive to do so. The situation is much worse when a serious reduction of household income coincides with a substantial decline in property value. The home owner not only faces immediate difficulty in making required mortgage payments, but she will also incur significant losses from a sale of the property, making default and foreclosure more likely. Waves of foreclosure are therefore more likely when both incomes and housing prices are falling throughout the economy.

The double trigger was activated during the 1930s because housing prices declined throughout the nation, millions of people lost jobs, and many who kept their jobs worked less and experienced declines in income. The situation has been similar during the recent housing crisis, although the income drops and unemployment shares are much smaller while the drops in housing prices in some of the major cities have been more spectacular. The 1930s and the first decade of the 2000s are the only decades in the past century to contain sustained nationwide drops in housing values. We will review each of these two triggers in turn.

INCOME

In terms of the income of mortgage borrowers, the Great Depression led to the greatest job loss and largest loss in per-person production of goods and services in American history. The timing of the increase in the unemployment rate matched the timing of the foreclosure crisis in figure 3.1. Unemployment spiked from 2.9 percent in 1929 to nearly 10 percent in 1930, and then kept rising to over 20 percent by 1932 and remained higher than 20 percent through 1935. By 1933 the number unemployed exceeded ten million people; nearly eight million of these people were not in the farm sector. Many who remained employed suffered income losses as average weekly hours worked fell from forty-eight to thirty-six, even though the purchasing power of hourly earnings held relatively steady between 1929 and 1933. Manufacturing workers saw their weekly earnings fall by 38 percent between 1929 and 1933. After accounting for the 20 percent decline in the general price level, their real purchasing power with weekly earnings had fallen 18 percent.[8]

Among nonfarm home owners in particular, the fall in income was likely as bad as these general figures, or possibly worse. In a survey of a large number of households across fifty cities in 1934, home owners saw an average decline in their family incomes of 36 percent between 1929 and 1933. After adjusting for deflation, a fall in the price level that made each dollar more valuable, their purchasing power fell 14 percent on average. Figure 3.2 shows the decline in real income after adjusting for deflation along the vertical axis. In forty-eight of the cities, real income declined at rates ranging from 1 percent in Columbia, South Carolina, to 37 percent in Racine, Wisconsin. Meanwhile, home

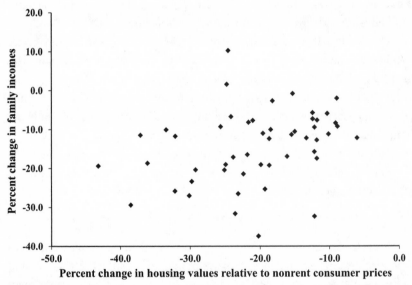

**Figure 3.2.** Changes in family incomes and housing values in fifty cities, 1929–1933. (Data from Wickens 1941, tables A10, C4.) Before calculating percentage changes, the family incomes were deflated using the national CPI series E-135 from US Bureau of the Census (1975, 211). The price index for nonrent consumer prices was calculated using the overall CPI (series E-135) and the rent CPI (series E-150) and assuming that rent accounted for 18 percent of the consumer budget.

owners in Binghamton, New York, and Jacksonville, Florida, experienced increases in real income.[9]

In terms of house prices, the same home owners from the fifty-city survey sample described sharp drops in their perceived resale values of their homes. Their housing values fell an average of 33 percent between 1930 and 1934. Other consumer prices were falling as well, but housing prices fell 20.5 percent more than nonhousing consumer prices over the four years. The declines from the peak prices in the late 1920s were probably greater still.[10]

Housing prices and incomes changed in different ways across different parts of the country. In figure 3.2, the changes in housing value (along the horizontal axis) varied across cities as much as the changes in income (along the vertical axis). For example, housing values dropped only 6 percent relative to other consumer prices in Portland, Maine, but fell by a much larger 43 percent in Wichita Falls, Texas. Borrowers living in the cities in the lower left part of figure 3.2, where income and house prices both dropped by the most, would most likely have trouble with foreclosure according to the double trigger framework.

Housing values may have fallen as much between 1930 and 1934 as they did between 2006 and 2010. As yet, only rough comparisons are possible because the earlier data are based on surveys of home owners about their housing values while most modern price indexes are based on actual market prices for homes. Three national price indexes for the modern period suggest average housing prices nationwide declined by as little as 16 percent or as much as 32 percent from their peak before the crisis to the end of 2010.[11] Housing prices relative to nonshelter consumer prices fell even more, because nonshelter consumer prices rose about 9 percent from 2006 to 2010. As a result, housing prices fell 25 to 41 percent more than nonshelter consumer prices over this period.

Mortgage borrowers during the early 1930s were not typically as indebted as their modern peers. Most first mortgage loans were limited to 50 or 60 percent of house value, and second mortgage loans likely brought indebtedness to about 80 percent at most for some borrowers. As a result, even with property tax debts that also often went unpaid in significant amounts during the 1930s, there were fewer borrowers during the early 1930s that were "underwater" in the modern vernacular, which means that they owed more than their houses were worth. We will present some more data along these lines in chapter 8 when we characterize the debt situation of HOLC borrowers. This point should not be overstated, as a number of home owners were indeed underwater, but compared to the crisis of the early 2000s, their numbers were relatively fewer.

When we talk about "market prices" in 1933, they should be interpreted as prices of transactions that actually occurred. This is an important caveat, as there was a broad credit crunch from 1932 to 1934. In most cases borrowers were able to sell their homes only if buyers could get credit. In some cases, buyers did get credit, and those transactions are the basis of market price estimates in those years. But the 1933 market was unpredictable, and some borrowers found buyers who were willing to pay "market price" in 1933 but then were not able to secure loans. Without credit the deal simply fell apart. As a result, there was a problem with the usual economic logic that suggests that prices would have fallen during the early 1930s until the market cleared. For the market to have cleared, prices would have needed to fall so substantially that most transactions could be accomplished on a cash basis without any new loans. Though the fall in prices was large during the 1930s, it was never large enough to allow all properties to transact, and borrowers would have had little interest in lowering their prices to a cash-only level. This helps explain why so many foreclosures occurred during the 1930s, despite the stricter loan-to-value ratios common during the 1920s. Borrowers could have escaped from their debts, avoiding the second part of the double trigger, only if credit was available either to them or to potential buyers.

The credit crunch jumps out of the data easily. In the late 1920s, lenders provided nearly $5 billion in new residential mortgage credit each year. By 1932, such lending fell to around $1 billion. Lending did not recover to even $2.5 billion until 1937.[12] This fall in loan volume reflected a lack of funds as well as a basic loss of creditworthiness on behalf of the nation's mortgage borrowers, given low incomes and housing prices that were in flux. This was a world without Fannie Mae and Freddie Mac buying up existing mortgages and freeing lenders to provide more mortgages. This is a key difference from the recent mortgage crisis.

## Borrowers' Trouble with Deflation

Home owners with mortgages in the early 1930s faced a severe problem with deflation in nonhousing prices that modern home owners have not faced.

Housing prices dropped from 2006 to 2010, but the overall price level rose 9 percent in the same period. In contrast, the consumer price index fell sharply between 1929 and 1933. This deflation meant that each dollar repaid by home borrowers to their lenders in 1933 contained 32.2 cents more in purchasing power than it had in 1929.

Prior to the 1930s, general deflations, with declines in both prices and wages, were considered to be part of the economy's normal adjustment process that would contribute to a return to economic expansions. The decline in prices was so rapid in the 1930s, however, that Irving Fisher, one of the leading economists of the day, pointed out an important flaw in the expectation that deflation would lead to a recovery. He argued that such a large fall in the general level of prices and wages during a time of extensive unemployment was actually destabilizing the economy because the value of the household debts rose. A few decades later Frederic Mishkin, who later served as a member of the Federal Reserve Board of Governors, showed how deflation sharply reduced the net wealth of households in the 1930s.[13]

For many people who kept their jobs, the general fall in prices and hourly wage rates did not reduce the purchasing power of hourly wages because consumer prices and hourly wages fell by roughly the same percentage between 1929 and 1933. However, a full-time worker with a home mortgage loan discovered that he was repaying the loan in dollars that were each worth 24 cents more than the dollars he had borrowed four years before. Thus, even though his flow of income in real terms was the same, the real cost of the payments on his debt had risen sharply. The situation was far worse for the mortgaged home owners who lost their jobs or found themselves working 20 to 25 percent fewer hours per week.

In sum, the double trigger model emphasizes that foreclosure becomes much more likely for an individual home owner when income loss is accompanied by a decrease in home values. In the 1930s both incomes and housing values fell for large shares of the population, causing a general foreclosure crisis. The problems were amplified further when deflation in nonhousing prices raised the real cost of repaying mortgage debts.

## The Downward Spiral

The wave of foreclosures contributed to a multifaceted downward spiral in the housing and real estate finance sectors. As the number of foreclosures rose above 200,000 per year (figure 3.1), they increasingly had negative effects on housing prices. Lower housing prices ate away at the equity of borrowers, making it difficult for them to settle their debts by selling their homes. Housing starts, shown in figure 2.1, declined to a low not otherwise seen after 1900, putting more construction workers out of work.

The basic business of real estate lenders fell apart. On one hand, lenders' real estate assets declined in value, and the fragility of balloon loans and share-accumulation loans became obvious. On the other hand, lenders' funds dried up. Partly, investors needed access to their savings, as the time from 1929 to 1933 was as rainy a day as they could have planned for. In addition, fears over losing money led many investors to pull funds. The net income of the life insurance industry was cut by more than half between 1929 and 1932 as nearly four times as many policies were cashed in for their surrender value and payments on disability claims rose. Commercial banks lost about one-third of their deposits. By 1933 nearly two thousand of the nation's roughly thirteen thousand B&Ls had failed, while members' savings in share accounts decreased by 25 percent.[14]

The credit crunch cemented the dysfunction in the housing market. Unless buyers could get credit, delinquent borrowers could not sell their homes without lowering prices so much that the housing market could operate on an all-cash basis. While prices did fall to some extent, and talk of a vast national "fire sale" of the nation's housing wealth increased, neither borrowers nor lenders had interest in selling properties at whatever price they could get. Credit rationing created large amounts of uncertainty as to what price could actually be obtained for any given property, depending on whether the potential buyer could get a loan. In this way, even borrowers with equity could not be assured of receiving the same price at which other similar houses had sold. As a result, lenders began stockpiling foreclosed assets on their books if they could avoid dumping them on the market, states passed foreclosure moratoria, and the housing market ceased to function in an orderly manner.

As the situation worsened, borrowers, lenders, and real estate professionals increasingly put pressure on government at all levels to do something about the crisis.

# CHAPTER 4

# PRESSURES
# FOR GOVERNMENT
# ACTION

---

The problems confronting the home owner cannot be exaggerated. His condition is most critical. The question as I see it is whether the Congress is going to stand by and see hundreds of thousands of honest citizens and their families turned out into the street, lose their life savings, because they are unable to renew mortgages upon their homes.
— Charles Cochran, Missouri, before the House of Representatives
   on April 25, 1933

I need not tax the patience of Members of the House in discussing the distressed conditions that obtain at this hour. They are recognized by all.
— Henry Steagall, Alabama, on introducing the Home Owners' Loan Act
   to the House of Representatives on April 27, 1933

Representatives Charles Cochran and Henry Steagall captured the mood of the nation's leaders in the spring of 1933.[1] It was apparent to all that the collapse of the mortgage market was creating a national crisis for borrowers and lenders alike. The establishment of the Federal Home Loan Bank system a year earlier had created hopes that the crisis would be eased, but ultimately the system was not the solution that the market needed. Meanwhile, more than half the states had established foreclosure moratorium laws that made it easier for home owners and farmers to hold on to their properties when they fell behind on making their mortgage payments. These measures were seen as temporary solutions with hopes that the Roosevelt administration and a newly elected Democratic Congress could help resolve the issues for the long run. The solution they came up with was the HOLC.

The HOLC relieved home owners by giving them a mechanism to avoid foreclosure and by adjusting their mortgage payments to the depressed economic circumstances. Roosevelt and his political allies emphasized this relief, and the bill had obvious appeal to voters on these grounds. The HOLC, like most New Deal programs, was designed to gain widespread public and political support while providing specific relief to target audiences. For the home mortgage market, this involved paying attention to the needs and expectations of mortgage lenders, real estate professionals, and home builders as well as to the home owners themselves. As we will see in later chapters, the mortgage lenders received relief from the HOLC because they were able to sell their troubled loans for HOLC bonds valued at or near the amount that was owed to them by the delinquent home owners. The size of the aid given mortgage lenders was not written into the law and came about as the HOLC administered its programs.

### State Mortgage Foreclosure Moratoria

Starting in the first months of 1933, twenty-seven states had implemented moratoria that attempted to curtail the downward pressure on home ownership and house prices by simply stopping the wave of foreclosures.[2] Several more states considered such laws. In many of these areas the statutes were passed to address distress among farm borrowers, while in several northeastern states trouble in urban areas played an important role.[3] In either case, nonfarm mortgagors as well as farm borrowers were covered. States used a variety of techniques to delay the ability of lenders to foreclose properties or to lengthen the periods during which borrowers could redeem their properties after foreclosure. Many states also passed legislation to discourage lenders from pursuing foreclosure by limiting access to deficiency judgments. These laws all generally challenged the contract clause of the US Constitution and so had to be rationalized by appealing to the emergency powers of state governments. The assertion of these emergency powers, also used in the context of the banking holidays declared around the same time, reflect the deep distress and dysfunction in credit markets at the time.

As solutions to the mortgage crisis, moratoria had three shortcomings. First, they were temporary measures to buy time and thus not responsive to the underlying decreases in income and house prices that were driving the foreclosure crisis. Second, they were all subject to judicial challenges because they interfered with private contracts. Many were struck down by state courts, and others (including the Minnesota moratorium that was upheld by the Supreme Court in the seminal Blaisdell case) were adjudicated all the way up to the federal level.[4] Third, the temporary assistance that the moratoria provided to borrowers could have led to unintended effects, including additional financial pressure on lenders and their ability to supply mortgage credit.[5]

The HOLC program addressed each of these shortcomings. It created a loan purchase and refinance program that brought mortgage payments in line with the lower levels of borrower income and home prices that had left hundreds of thousands of home owners facing imminent foreclosure in 1933. The sanctity of private contracts was protected because the loan could be modified only after both borrower and lender agreed to participate. Finally, the HOLC's purchase of the loan from the lender replaced the troubled loan with a risk-free HOLC bond that improved the lender's probability of survival.

### Federal Intervention before the HOLC

In December 1931 President Hoover responded to the mounting mortgage crisis by convening a national conference on home building and home ownership. Hoover unveiled a proposal at the conference for the creation of a federally sponsored home loan bank system to facilitate the long-run goal of increasing home ownership and to address the immediate emergency in the housing market. Congress created the Federal Home Loan Bank (FHLB) system on July 22, 1932. Mimicking the structures of the Federal Land Bank system (established in 1916) and the Federal Reserve System (established in 1913), the act created a system of twelve regional banks with a supervisory board in Washington, DC, which has survived and evolved to this day. Its beginnings were troubled, though, as it had little success in stemming the foreclosure crisis in the Depression. The FHLB system's failure to stem the housing crisis offers insights into the problems that made collective action by lenders' groups without the HOLC difficult to achieve.

Each of the twelve FHLBs was empowered to make loans, called advances, to member financial institutions. The collateral on these advances, assets pledged to one of the FHLBs, were the mortgage loans held by the financial institutions. These advances were designed to provide mortgage lenders with more funds that would allow them to make additional mortgage loans. The advances also could help lenders get cash quickly when they faced short-run financial strains. By providing cash in emergencies, the regional FHLBs were serving the same purpose for mortgage lenders that the regional Federal Reserve Banks served for commercial banks. A program that provides loans of this type is typically described as a "discount facility." Through such a facility, the FHLB potentially had the laudable effect of stabilizing mortgage lending, which, in turn, could help stabilize home prices and increase production and employment in the home-building industry.

The FHLB discount facility, however, did not have much to offer to lenders already burdened by bad loans or lenders who were facing long-run financial strain. Only loans in good standing could be used as collateral for loans from the system. This made it difficult for the lenders in the most trouble to qualify as FHLB members, and without membership they had no access to the discount facility. Even members of the FHLB system had to be careful in making new loans because the FHLB would not lend to them if they accumulated too large a share of problem loans and put their long-term viability at risk. Altogether, the FHLBs were designed to provide cash to those short of liquidity, but the system did not deal with troubled loans or provide capital to lenders on troubled loans.[6]

In addition, the FHLB's impact was limited because it generally worked with only one of the most important lender groups. Although Hoover had envisioned an FHLB system that served all institutional residential mortgage lenders, leaders of the B&L movement—who had lobbied for a system like the FHLB system for more than decade—succeeded in limiting the FHLB system to just B&Ls. Life insurance companies, mutual savings banks, commercial banks, and other lenders combined accounted for about the same amount of lending on residential mortgages as B&Ls, and were largely left out of the FHLB system. As a result, an effective solution involving all residential home lenders had not been tried by 1933.

The FHLB system possessed one final tool to address the mortgage market's problems. The FHLB Act gave the FHLB system the ability to make direct loans to the hundreds of thousands of home owners who had fallen behind on their mortgage payments in the early 1930s. In a remarkable bout of inaction, the FHLBs never made a single loan under this authority. FHLB officials blamed their inactivity on the infeasibility of such a program, such as the administrative difficulties of creating a new lending program. There was also much confusion about whether loans could be made only in areas that were not already served by existing FHLB members. These protestations have some merit, yet it seems clear that FHLB officials had little interest in making direct loans to residential mortgage borrowers, and they were quite relieved when that power was transferred to the HOLC after less than a year. As a result, during the debate over the Home Owners' Loan Bill in the spring of 1933, many congressmen expressed frustration and outrage that the FHLB had done so little and sought assurance that the HOLC would not have a similar record. These sentiments are exemplified in a speech by Representative John Cochran of Missouri:

> We passed a bill in the last session which we were told was for the relief of the home owners. We created a home-loan bank, and what was it? It was nothing but a political fraud, and up to this hour not one single individual in this country has been able to get 5 cents from that home-loan bank to retire a mortgage. It was a bill for the relief of building-and-loan associations. The bill which is to be considered now should be a real relief bill for home owners in the large cities. We have given everything to the farmers, we have given everything to the corporations, but what have we done for the man who owns a little home in the city, representing his life savings?[7]

The FHLB was the last major piece of legislation during the Hoover administration. The HOLC bill was passed during the first hundred days of the Roosevelt administration as part of its effort to deal with a wide range of problems created by the Great Depression.

## The Passage of the HOLC

The HOLC was one of many programs that Franklin Roosevelt and a newly Democratic Congress enacted to address the crumbling economy in their first hundred days in office. The Federal Emergency Relief Administration, Civilian Conservation Corps, and Public Works Administration provided direct relief payments and jobs for millions of unemployed. The Agricultural Adjustment Act and farm credit legislation provided aid to farmers facing declining incomes and farm foreclosures. The Reconstruction Finance Corporation made loans and took ownership stakes in hundreds of banks under the Hoover administration, and then provided extensive aid to hundreds of industrial firms and dozens of railroads under Roosevelt. National bank holidays, the move off the gold standard, new banking regulations, the Federal Deposit Insurance Corporation, and new Federal Reserve policies helped save commercial banks and restructure the system. The National Recovery Administration was meant to help industry and workers by raising wages and prices.

The New Dealers sought to provide aid to nearly all parts of society. Therefore, it would have been unusual if they had ignored the residential mortgage crisis. In the HOLC's case, a number of different constituencies combined to support the legislation. Home owners were the constituents most likely to vote in elections, and lenders and urban real estate professionals had active lobbies that pressed for continued aid. Their lobbying efforts gained strength from the early passage of the farm credit legislation that reorganized the aid provided to farm mortgages. President Roosevelt and numerous legislators had every reason to champion a program to aid distressed home owners and lenders.

EMPATHY FOR HOME OWNERS AND THEIR
STRENGTH AT THE BALLOT BOX

Distressed home owners and their neighbors had clout in elections because they were the ones turning out to vote and making small contributions to political campaigns. Politicians ignored that clout at their peril.

Public speeches advocating for the HOLC focused primarily on the importance of protecting home owners from the widespread and acute foreclosure crisis described in chapter 3. This was similar to the justifications used by the Roosevelt administration and Congress to promote a constellation of other New Deal relief programs. When the president submitted the draft HOLC legislation to Congress, in the accompanying message he emphasized how the legislation would provide home owners with relief: "As a further and urgently necessary step in the program to promote economic recovery, I ask the Congress for legislation to protect small home owners from foreclosure and to relieve them of a portion of the burden of excessive interest and principal payments incurred during the period of higher values and higher earning power."[8]

President Roosevelt's message to Congress additionally emphasized that the HOLC was specifically intended "to protect the small home owner." The proposed bill restricted the program to homes that were valued at no more than $10,000, but the limit excluded only about 15 percent of nonfarm home owners in the 1930 census. In the final version of the bill, the maximum limit was raised to $20,000 at the behest of the greater New York City congressional delegation, who pointed out that between one-third and one-half of their constituents who owned homes were excluded by the original $10,000 limit. Under the final $20,000 limit, only 3.4 percent of the nation's home owners were excluded from the program. Altogether, the HOLC was accessible to all but the most affluent home owners in the country.[9]

To preempt complaints that the HOLC was helping affluent Americans, President Roosevelt noted the unfairness imposed on debtors in a time of deflation and poor economic prospects. He asserted it was inherently "inequitable" for home owners to be allowed to suffer "enforced liquidation, in a time of general distress." He went even further by outlining a moral framework to underpin the need for federal intervention: "Implicit in the legislation which I am suggesting to you, is a declaration of national policy. This policy is that the broad interests of the nation require that special safeguards should be thrown around home ownership as a guaranty of social and economic stability, and that to protect home owners from inequitable enforced liquidation, in a time of general distress, is a proper concern of the Government."

Roosevelt's moral framework therefore created a momentous and far-reaching argument for the HOLC. It argued that not only *could* the federal government give relief to home mortgage borrowers, but that it *should* do so, given the circumstances prevailing in the Depression.

The HOLC continued to emphasize these ideas after it had been established. HOLC annual reports perennially noted that its mission was "to aid a class of home owners in hard straits largely through no fault of their own."[10] Such characterizations were unlikely to be disputed by anybody who had tried to get a home loan. To get a loan in the 1920s required a hefty down payment of 40 or 50 percent of the value of the house, and a second mortgage could be obtained only by paying an interest rate of 11 or 12 percent. These were conservative loans that were dependable in normal times. Many of the problems developed only after people lost jobs or could not obtain new loans because the lenders were struggling as well. Many borrowers were pushed into default when they tried to follow the standard procedure of renewing the loan when the principal came due, and discovered the lender did not have the funds to renew.

In the environment of the 1930s, empathy for families in danger of losing their homes in foreclosure was not hard to come by. By 1933, incomes had fallen sharply in households in all parts of the income distribution.[11] Many home owners saw their neighbors facing possible loss of their home and thought that they might well face the same situation soon. They expressed these fears in a variety of ways. Each Monday night in the spring of 1933, one thousand people met in a New York church to pray for home owners who were threatened by foreclosure. These developments created a powerful political coalition among voters for the passage of the HOLC.[12]

## ROOSEVELT COULD NOT HELP FARMERS WITHOUT SIMILAR AID TO HOME OWNERS

The case for aid to home owners was bolstered by the passage of legislation in mid-May, about two months after Roosevelt took office, to address problems with farm mortgages. J. Marvin Jones, a Texas Democrat who headed the House Agriculture Committee, introduced a bill for federal refinancing of farm mortgages on February 18, 1933, two weeks before Roosevelt was inaugurated.[13] Roosevelt began to address the issue soon after taking office. When he submitted the Emergency Farm Mortgage Act to Congress on April 3, his message emphasized that the bill was designed to provide farmers with reasonable loan terms to "lighten their harassing burdens and give them a fair opportunity to return to sound conditions." This reasoning anticipates much of the framework Roosevelt used later that spring to urge passage of the HOLC.

The farm foreclosure crisis had started much earlier than its residential counterpart, with a genesis in the rapid expansion in mortgage debt during the World War I–era US agricultural boom. In 1920, as the demand for US farm products fell back to normal levels, a surge of farm foreclosures began. Foreclosures remained elevated even in the second half of the 1920s.[14] The federal government was heavily invested in the farm mortgage problems because it supported a network of cooperative lending agencies, the Federal Land Banks, and supervised a system of privately owned farm mortgage joint-stock banks, all set up by Congress in 1916. By 1930 these two sets of lenders held about one-fifth of the nation's farm mortgage debt.[15] In 1932, 4.2 percent of farm mortgages ended in either foreclosure or forced sale due to tax debt, up from 2.0 to 2.5 percent in each year since 1926. Altogether, from

1926 to 1942, 17.5 percent of farm mortgages were transferred by foreclosure or forced sale. The Federal Land Banks were bailed out by cash infusions from Congress in February 1932, and the joint-stock banking system faced imminent collapse by 1933.[16]

In a sign of the times, life insurance companies—the largest private farm mortgage lenders—had voluntarily suspended foreclosures so that they could avoid seizing and managing even more farmland than they already had.[17] The situation was analogous to that in the home mortgage sector, with lending activity at a standstill and lenders looking to the federal government for a solution.[18]

When proposing the farm mortgage relief bill, Roosevelt noted that he would "presently ask for additional legislation . . . extending this wholesome principle to the small home owners of the nation." Later that spring, when Roosevelt sent to Congress the HOLC bill, he again noted that "the legislation I propose follows the general lines of the farm mortgage refinancing bill." Fundamentally, the genesis, design, and political success of the HOLC were joined at the hip to the federal government's response to the parallel farm mortgage crisis.[19]

## LOBBYING BY LENDERS AND REAL ESTATE PROFESSIONALS

The federal government's action to establish the HOLC followed months of lobbying by urban mortgage lenders and real estate professionals throughout the country.[20] Lenders had become disenchanted with the FHLB system. They considered it inadequate to the task of dealing with the crisis, particularly because it ignored so many of the troubled lenders other than B&Ls. Even though many lenders had supported state-level measures, such as mortgage moratoria, to deal with the mortgage crisis, each measure was often seen as "a temporary measure . . . until some national legislation is formulated, either by liberalizing the Home Loan Bank System or establishing a Mortgage Bank of Discount."[21] Compared to the general public, lenders and real estate professionals had the advantage of being able to organize as a special interest in lobbying government. They were easier to organize because they had more focused interests and each had more at stake from the passage of a specific law. They represented an important voice, therefore, in policy formulation.

The nonfarm real estate industry proposals generally focused on three major principles in developing the solution to the foreclosure crisis. First,

many emphasized the importance of reducing foreclosures through voluntary, cooperative action between borrower and lender rather than legislative
mandates. Second, to facilitate these voluntary resolutions, there was widespread support for lower interest rates and liberal extensions for principal
repayments as resolution mechanisms. The idea of reducing the principal
on loans, however, was virtually never mentioned. One commentator who at
least broached the subject listed principal reduction as a last and a "drastic"
solution to foreclosure resolution of defaults on property taxes.[22]

Third, the professional real estate community provided active support
for resolution of the wave of property tax delinquencies that accompanied
mortgage defaults. Lenders, even with first mortgage liens, had junior claims
to local tax authorities in the event of foreclosure and could not effect loan
modifications with their borrowers without addressing a tax delinquency.[23] In
his study of the property tax revolt of the early 1930s, David Beito character-
izes the National Association of Real Estate Boards (NAREB) as the "closest
facsimile" to a national organization in the movement.[24] The broad coalition
supporting the HOLC therefore also likely included local governments.

The design and implementation of the HOLC followed all three of these
principles. We will discuss the HOLC's refinancing terms in detail in chapters 5 and 6, but note some key features here in the context of what lenders and real estate professionals had proposed. First, in line with the call for
voluntary action, the HOLC had no power to compel lenders to cooperate.
The HOLC had to purchase each loan from the lender that owned it before it
could offer refinancing. The HOLC paid values in bonds that typically covered
the lion's share of the full amount owed to the lender. Second, HOLC interest
rates were lower than prevailing rates on private loans, durations were longer,
and the HOLC also offered an optional three-year period during which only
interest payments were required. Finally, the HOLC worked diligently with
lenders and borrowers to cover tax payments and avoid loss of the property to
local governments.

In the end, the HOLC was supported by nonfarm home owners, who had
power at the ballot box, along with lenders and urban real estate interests,
who were a powerful lobby. This combination, along with the argument that
home owners in trouble should be aided if the government was helping everybody else, clearly bore fruit. The HOLC Act passed the House of Representatives 383–4 and on a voice vote in the Senate on June 13, 1933.[25]

# CHAPTER 5

# THE ECONOMIC
# RATIONALE FOR
# THE HOLC

What is the economic rationale underlying the HOLC's intervention into the residential loan market? This is a question of whether the program can be justified from an economic policy perspective, rather than how Congress and the president actually justified it. Not all distressed loans are good candidates for modifications, but society is often better off if lenders choose to modify some distressed loans rather than foreclose upon them. From this perspective, the important question for policy is why lenders chose to foreclose so many loans during the 1930s rather than implement HOLC-style modifications themselves. Moreover, if borrowers, lenders, and the economy as a whole were better off with so many loan modifications, we must also consider why private actors did not come together to create a private version of the HOLC.

## Foreclosure as a Resolution Mechanism

During normal periods foreclosures are relatively rare events, and the problems of foreclosure are dealt with in a routine fashion. The possibility for foreclosure is included in all mortgage contracts to provide a solution, agreed upon at the time the contract was signed, that can be used to resolve a lender's claims if the borrower defaults on scheduled loan payments.[1] Foreclosure clauses establish the procedures for selling a mortgaged property to pay off any remaining loan balance, any unpaid interest, and any costs the lender incurs while pursuing foreclosure and the property sale.

Foreclosure is a key incentive for borrowers to pay back their loans and a way for lenders to reduce losses in cases when borrowers do not repay. Nevertheless, the foreclosure option is often not used because it is more costly than other solutions for resolving a default. Foreclosure requires time, effort, and legal fees to remove the borrower's ownership rights to a property. It then generates expenses related to the sale of the property, including possible costs of repairs if the borrower did not maintain the home.

In the event of borrower default, there are two possible cases: the property can be sold for either more or less than the lender's claims plus the costs of selling the property. When the property can be sold for more, the borrower has an incentive to avoid foreclosure and its costs, and therefore retain more of her equity, by simply selling the property herself and repaying the lender with the proceeds.

If the sale of the property cannot fully cover all the lender's claims, on the other hand, the burden of foreclosure costs shifts to the lender. In this situation, both borrowers and lenders can often do better through modification of the defaulted loan rather than foreclosing upon the borrower. This approach lets the borrower stay in the home with an opportunity to resolve the default without generating the costs associated with transferring ownership and selling the property. By modifying the loan, moreover, the lender avoids the costs of holding and managing the borrower's property if it turns out to be hard to sell. It also gives the borrower more incentive to maintain the property because she retains ownership so long as she can meet the requirements of the modified loan.

### Why Lenders Did Not Implement HOLC-Style Modifications during the 1930s

Lenders in the early 1930s were well aware of the benefits of loan modification after a default rather than foreclosure. In New York City, research on property prices during the 1920s and 1930s shows that the sale price for foreclosed property was about 26 percent lower than the sale price for similar properties in regular sales. Lenders expected, therefore, that there would be fewer resources to pay off debts after a foreclosure. A major factor in these costs was delay. In a sample of New York mortgages from 1920 through 1947, the average time between the date the lender dispatched the loan to a foreclosure attorney and the completion of the foreclosure was around five months. On average, it took the lender about 4.7 years to sell the property, although many lenders were able to rent out the homes while waiting to sell them. As a result, foreclosures were neither a fast nor a low-risk way to obtain cash when a lender ran into trouble.[2]

Faced with these practicalities, lenders commonly modified loans rather than foreclosing, even as the mortgage crisis heated up between 1931 and 1933. In a study of New York mortgages during that time, lenders modified an annual average of 8 percent of the loans in place, while they foreclosed on only 1.1 percent. These modifications were not as concessionary as HOLC modifications, however, nor were they as effective. The structure of these modifications followed the pattern advocated publicly by lenders' groups for the HOLC. Over 96 percent of the modifications lengthened the repayment period, 40 percent changed the type of loan, and only 10 percent lowered the interest rate. Literally none of the modifications lowered the principal debt, and in some modifications the borrower ended up with worse terms than before.[3]

Despite the costs and delays associated with foreclosure, the number of foreclosures nationwide increased by roughly 65 percent between 1930 and 1932. The number of foreclosures threatened to grow so large that various states began to implement foreclosure moratoria. The most obvious reason for the rise in foreclosures would seem to have been that more borrowers were falling behind on their mortgages as the economy crumbled. Yet lenders still might have handled the problems with modifications instead of foreclosures. Instead, in the New York sample, the ratio of foreclosures to modifications rose each year from 1932 through 1935.[4]

Modifications were even more difficult in situations where multiple lenders owned the loan or where there was a second mortgage on the property. Not only were the basic negotiation costs amplified by having multiple lenders, but there was a greater likelihood of disagreement between the mortgage lenders, and legal safeguards put in place to protect each lender created additional obstacles. This became a particularly severe problem in the New York and Chicago metropolitan areas, where mortgage guarantee companies had issued mortgage-backed securities based on groups of mortgages and sometimes sold pieces of the same mortgage to multiple investors. The mortgage companies that issued and guaranteed these securities failed during the foreclosure crisis, and special legislative solutions were required to obtain permission for modification from dispersed investors. A relatively small share of mortgages were involved in these transactions, so the problem was not as severe as in the recent mortgage crisis when most mortgages were included as parts of securities.[5]

In choosing between modification and foreclosure, a lender would typically compare the cash flow from the two options. To put dollars earned in the future on the same terms as dollars earned sooner, lenders discount future cash flows, resulting in a net present value (NPV) for each option. The cash flows are quite different for foreclosures and modifications. Foreclosures have some upfront costs and a lump-sum cash flow whenever the property is sold, though the gap before sales may be long. For example, a federal government study estimated that the duration of the foreclosure process averaged eight months across the forty-eight states during the 1930s. The survey also noted some significant expenses from legal fees, court costs, and advertising.[6] Although foreclosure raises funds at a delay of several months, the discounted cash flow could still be higher than a modification. At best, modifications bring lenders revenue only gradually as loan payments are made, and at worst modifications can just end in redefaults. The total cash flow may be higher than a foreclosure, but once receipts many years in the future are discounted, the NPV may be lower. As a result, whether the NPV of a modification exceeds that of a foreclosure depends very much on the rate at which future cash flow is discounted, and on the probability of redefault.

If a lender did an NPV test for a modification in 1933, the lender likely thought a great deal about the borrower's ability to pay off the loan amid the Depression. As unemployment rose and there appeared to be no end in sight, lenders faced increasing difficulty in accurately identifying viable candidates for modification. Modification made sense if borrowers were likely to eventually repay their loans, but expanding unemployment (and underemployment) made it more difficult to identify which borrowers were in a situation where they might return to work in a reasonable time span. Lenders were reluctant to extend modifications to borrowers who would default in the future regardless of the modification. As a result, many NPV tests likely favored foreclosure on solid economic grounds.

However, not all lender NPV tests are necessarily optimal from a societal point of view. Society's NPVs may differ from lenders' NPVs in many cases. Consider three reasons why lenders might view a modification as having an NPV that is "too low." First, there are costs of foreclosure that are imposed on society and not on a lender, which often caused lenders to disregard these costs. Second, because of the distressed conditions of the early 1930s, lenders might have been using particularly high discount rates when considering the value of revenue several years in the future, making modifications less attractive. Third, lenders may have valued modifications less because of concerns that nondistressed borrowers would seek modifications as well, if a program like the HOLC had any greater ability to prevent such concerns, which it might not.

## SOCIAL COSTS OF FORECLOSURES

Several costs to foreclosure are not internalized by lenders but instead are borne by others. This is especially true when the number of foreclosures becomes large. As foreclosure sales move from relatively rare events to more common ones, they are more likely to have important impacts on house prices. Moreover, individual lenders have little incentive to consider these costs, as most lenders are too small to affect aggregate housing prices even within a community. In the 1930s, as the number of foreclosures mounted, each foreclosure created negative spillover effects on all home sales. A leading real estate professional noted the problem at the height of the 1930s foreclosure crisis: "Foreclosures in this situation are destructive to the market in general. They accomplish nothing of lasting benefit, even to the holder of the mortgage . . . since the effect of forced sales is [to] demoralize values in the vicinity and therefore to depreciate that of his acquisition."[7] The individual lender had every incentive to focus on his own benefits and costs, including the demoralizing effect on the price of his own foreclosed property, and ignore the spillover effects on other values in the vicinity.

As housing prices fell further, borrowers found it even more difficult to sell homes to meet the demands of lenders, putting more people in danger of falling behind on their payments. More people pulled deposits out of banks and savings institutions, and fewer people bought insurance, further cutting the funds with which lenders could make loans. As the supply of credit dried up, the housing market went into a downward spiral of decreases in home values, additional home foreclosures, further deterioration in household balance sheets, and further disruptions in intermediated mortgage lending channels. Economists refer to this situation as the "financial accelerator," and historians have argued that this force was at work not only during the mortgage crisis of the early 1930s but in other crises as well.[8] The individual lender bears the burden of only the losses on his own foreclosed property and not the spillover costs on other properties. In addition, foreclosure imposes costs on neighborhoods through the blight of unoccupied homes, and on families through the stress of losing their homes.

These are costs that are not reflected in individual lenders' NPV tests between modification and foreclosure. As a result, society as a whole might have an interest in arranging for more modifications than lenders would enact on their own, and might be willing to spend taxpayer money in the process.[9] No individual lender would have the incentive to take these concerns into account, and collective action among lenders would be quite difficult, as individual lenders would have a strong incentive to defect from any agreement against foreclosure. No individual lender had the ability to stop the collapse of the real estate market, nor to contribute much to the collapse by dumping one more foreclosed property on the market.

In contrast, since the HOLC controlled such a large part of the loan market, its policies were much more likely to potentially affect aggregate market prices. The HOLC was large enough to interrupt the fire-sale atmosphere in the residential real estate market of the mid-1930s. Moreover, it could do so without the collective action problems that private lenders would face. In general, the HOLC was designed to take spillover costs into account when evaluating whether a modification should be pursued rather than a foreclosure.

DISCOUNT RATES

Modifications yield income streams that are drawn out and uncertain given the possibility of redefault. As a result, lenders are more likely to enact modifications if they are patient and do not discount future cash flows too heavily. Lenders in 1933 could not afford much patience, however. Lenders were under pressure to shrink their lending during the early 1930s as funding became increasingly scarce. Between 1929 and 1933, the supply of loanable funds declined consistently, and after 1933 these funds came back only slowly. These declines occurred over several years, not just panic-driven withdrawals over short periods. B&Ls, for example, usually did not have to pay all withdrawals on demand, but rather could use available cash to pay some portion of withdrawals each month. In such cases, withdrawals were not satisfied for years. Over the same period, depositors steadily withdrew their funds from savings banks and commercial banks, and policyholders cashed in their accounts at life insurance companies. To make up the difference, all of these lenders borrowed what they could from other sources and liquidated investments such as securities when possible, but eventually contraction of loan portfolios was needed to rebalance assets and liabilities.

These funding declines likely raised lenders' discount rates, as they were more likely to value activities that generated cash flow sooner rather than later. There is little way to measure how lenders' preferences changed, but it is difficult to believe that the lenders' patience rose, and much easier to imagine lenders becoming more impatient with loans in default. When lenders conducted NPV tests, though foreclosures did not generate immediate cash flow, lenders might see that cash flow from foreclosure could easily be faster than that of a modification. With a large enough discount rate, foreclosure could be preferred, as a lender with large withdrawal demands over, say, a two-year period, would value very little income coming five years later.

In effect, illiquidity—the lack of cash to meet obligations—can prevent lenders from making good investments, as the high discount rate would lower some investments' discounted cash flows. Fundamentally, lenders' high discount rates during the 1930s stemmed from an interruption in the ability of lenders to mediate between borrowers and savers. After 1929 the supply of savings available to traditional private real estate lenders simply declined in aggregate, as households and businesses became less likely to accumulate new savings and more likely to tap into their existing savings to replace lost income. Therefore, in order to sustain the same level of activity, existing lenders would have needed to find new sources of funding, but they were in no way prepared for such a fundamental and rapid change. No new private-sector intermediaries popped up to fill the void.

The HOLC directly filled this void by tapping a new class of investors who were willing to invest in the HOLC and therefore supply credit to borrowers. This effectively increased the amount of funding that was available for residential mortgage lending by breaking free from the traditional funding sources relied upon by existing lenders, who simply did not have access to the HOLC's form of financing. In fact, this is a key traditional role of a bad bank. Bad banks allow troubled assets to be segregated away from other assets, funded differently, and therefore dealt with patiently, free from the pressures faced by lenders with credit-quality problems funded by impatient investors or depositors.

As noted in chapter 4, the FHLB system was also created to help address the funding shortfall, but failed. There were several shortcomings in the FHLB, including that its activities were limited to B&Ls in relatively strong condition. Fundamentally, though, the FHLB system had only about $85 million in loans to lenders outstanding at the end of 1933 and 1934. In comparison, the HOLC funded $3 billion in loans between 1933 and 1936. The FHLB simply did not match the scale of the shortfall in funds available for lending, and therefore likely did not have the ability to materially lower lenders' discount rates or change their NPV tests.

## ISOLATING GOOD PROSPECTS FOR MODIFICATION

Lenders likely worried about extending modifications to borrowers who were not truly in distress. For example, if a lender set benchmarks for borrowers to meet in order to obtain a modification, such as delinquency for three months, borrowers would have a strategic opportunity to obtain a modification.[10] They could stop paying for a while, meet the benchmark, and obtain a modification. Meanwhile, losses from the unnecessary modification could further weaken the lenders. No lender wants to give concessions to borrowers who do not need them, or to borrowers who are likely to default even with the concessions. Such information problems could lower the NPV of a modification, and anecdotes from the 1930s suggest this was the case, although there is little systematic evidence.

These information problems are difficult to solve, and the HOLC had no silver bullet. The Roosevelt administration emphasized the HOLC as a relief program for home owners who ran into problems "through no fault of their own." To identify such borrowers, it seems unlikely that the HOLC had any more information than existing lenders. The HOLC ran credit reports on borrowers and asked about their employment situation, but lenders had the ability to do the same and had the entire loan case file at their disposal.

The HOLC's application structure might have helped. The HOLC was able to mitigate moral hazard somewhat by requiring (as of an April 1934 amendment) that borrowers' defaults be dated to before the HOLC's establishment in June 1933.[11] The HOLC's structure might also have helped mitigate the problems of identifying truly distressed borrowers. The HOLC accepted applications for limited windows from May 1933 to November 1934, and then in May and June 1935. This could have prevented nondistressed borrowers from gaming the system by imitating the characteristics of successful applicants.

The law establishing the HOLC also created criminal penalties for anyone who misrepresented information to the organization, a fact that was noted in HOLC literature for the public, though it is not clear that any loan applicants were ever prosecuted under that law.

Each application took several months to process; therefore, relatively few borrowers would have had enough information about the true benefits of the modifications before filing applications. The corporation tried to discourage applications by publicizing their rejection rate of nearly 50 percent. By fall 1933 the agency regularly reported in newspapers the number of applicants who had been rejected because they did not meet the program's eligibility requirements or could not demonstrate sufficient distress.[12]

Over several years, the HOLC did eventually figure out which borrowers had no hope of meeting their debts. Essentially, the HOLC gathered information by implementing modifications and carefully monitoring who was likely to redefault. Such cases ended in foreclosure, and ultimately constituted nearly 20 percent of their pool of borrowers. The average loss on these foreclosures was 33 percent. One way of looking at the program is whether the benefits delivered to the 80 percent of borrowers who did not foreclose were worth the losses incurred on the remaining loans.

## Could the HOLC Have Been Done Privately?

The HOLC was a government-sponsored bad bank. The HOLC bought large numbers of troubled loans from the lenders at or near the full value of the loans, and then took control of restructuring and servicing the loans. Whenever the government intervenes into the private market as the HOLC did, a natural question is why no private actors were interested in providing whatever service the government provides. There is no evidence from the early 1930s that any group of private actors considered creating a private version of the HOLC, but we discuss why this was not the case as a way of clarifying the HOLC's role in the economy.

A bad bank, either public or private, had several potential advantages in dealing with the foreclosure crisis relative to individual mortgage lenders acting on their own. First, no single lender was large enough to resolve the problems of the foreclosure crisis, so some form of collective action, either by an association of private lenders or by the government, was necessary to stop the downward spiral that was afflicting the mortgage and housing markets in

1933. By controlling a large share of the loan market, a bad bank could have the incentive and the capacity to take into account the spillover problems associated with foreclosure sales, and therefore reduce the number of foreclosures and slow the pace of foreclosed property sales.

Second, with long-term funding, the bad bank would not have to worry about the problems of carrying illiquid and nonperforming loans while being unable to meet withdrawal demands. The HOLC, for example, reduced these mismatch problems by issuing bonds, in 1933 and 1934, with maturity dates of 1949–1951.[13] The HOLC, therefore, could be patient in waiting for the foreclosure crisis to subside without fear of bondholders demanding earlier repayment. Meanwhile, the corporation had a substantial flow of principal and interest payments coming in each year from the refinanced loans it owned, and so could be lenient with borrowers facing foreclosure.

Third, a sufficiently large bad bank could diversify the risk of modifying troubled loans by assembling a portfolio of loans purchased from many lenders who operated in different local markets. Compared to an individual lender, a bad bank would have a more diversified portfolio funded over a longer term, potentially allowing it to raise capital at lower interest rates and for longer periods than a single lender.

All of these advantages apply to either a public or a private bad bank. Private lenders could have come together to form their own bad bank, or a group of private investors could have pooled capital to form a bad bank. It is important to understand what prevented them from doing so, and what relative advantages a publicly sponsored bad bank would have had. No bad bank can operate without funding, so a key to success is the ability to raise funds for purchasing loans. Any private bad bank would first have to gather investors who would be willing to invest capital in the enterprise and risk taking the first losses but also any potential profits. Such capital was likely quite scarce in the mid-1930s. Alternatively, a group of existing lenders could pool their loans, but a funding source would still have to be arranged. Assuming capital could be put in place, the bad bank would then try to raise additional funds, perhaps through bond issuance like the HOLC. An important issue, therefore, would be what interest rates market participants would demand in exchange for investing in such risky bonds, if they could be induced to invest in such bonds at all.

Government guarantees gave the HOLC a substantial advantage in raising enough funds to purchase the troubled loans. When the HOLC first issued bonds in 1933, only the interest was guaranteed, but this was enough of a guarantee that the HOLC could issue bonds at the same interest rate as on high-grade corporate bonds with the same maturity. Once the federal government guaranteed the principal as well, HOLC bonds were equivalent to Treasury bonds, and their interest rates fell to 1 percentage point below the rates on high-grade corporate bonds.[14]

If a private bad bank had issued bonds to finance the purchase of loans, the interest rate on the bonds would have had to reflect the risk of loss from operating the bad bank. This risk, in turn, was determined by the probability that the bad bank would have to foreclose on the loans as well as the costs for each foreclosure. We estimate that the rate on bonds issued for a private bad bank likely would have been 1 to 3 percentage points higher than on HOLC bonds. The HOLC ended up foreclosing on 20 percent of the loans it bought and refinanced, and auditors estimated that the average loss on each foreclosure was around 30 percent. Calculations based on this information suggest that an investor who was "risk neutral" would have demanded an interest rate on the private bad bank bonds that was at least 1.25 percentage points higher than the rate on guaranteed HOLC bonds.[15] The 1.25 percentage points can be described as a "risk premium," which is the difference between the interest rates on a risk-free investment and on a risky investment that would have made the investor equally willing to invest in either investment. Had investors expected the private bad bank to foreclose on 30 percent of its troubled loans rather than the 20 percent by the HOLC, the risk premium for a risk-neutral investor would have risen to roughly 2 percent. Uncertainty about the risks of the loans would have raised the demanded risk premium even further. Few people at the time could have predicted effectively what share of the loans could be rescued. Investors react to such uncertainty by seeking additional risk premiums that could have raised the rate nearly 3 percent or more above the risk-free rate.

One reason that the private bad bank foreclosure rate would likely have exceeded the HOLC's rate is that the HOLC refinanced the borrowers' loans at a 5 percent interest rate, even though the original mortgages were issued at interest rates ranging from 6 to 8 percent. Expert testimony by Horace Russell on April 20, 1933, shows that the HOLC was expected to lose money at the 5 percent interest rate. Russell was the Roosevelt administration's point man in selling the legislation to Congress. As general counsel to the Federal Home Loan Bank Board, he also was heavily involved in drafting the bill. He confronted the issue of the expected profitability of the HOLC in a remarkably candid exchange with two Republicans on the Senate Banking Committee, John Townsend of Delaware and James Crouzens of Michigan.

> SENATOR TOWNSEND. And you figure on this set-up that you have in the provisions of this bill that the Government would not lose any money?
>
> MR. RUSSELL. Senator, I think that the rate [on mortgage loans] ought to be 6 percent in this bill, and if it were 6 percent, in my judgment the government would not lose any money, but at 5 percent my best judgment is that it cannot be operated at all on a 1 percent spread [between the mortgage rate and the HOLC bond rate]. Nobody else has ever been successful in operating a first-mortgage business of this character on a 1 percent spread.
>
> SENATOR TOWNSEND. If you thought it ought to be 6 percent, why did you make it 5?
>
> MR. RUSSELL. Well, I made it 6 and it was changed.
>
> SENATOR CROUZENS. So far as I am concerned, I am perfectly willing that the Government should lose some money. . . .
>
> MR. RUSSELL. [Interposing] That was the theory of that change.

When the HOLC first issued its bonds in 1933 with a federal government guarantee of only interest payments, the interest rate was 4 percent. Horace Russell suggested that the HOLC might have made money by charging 2 percent more to borrowers when refinancing the loans but would have lost money by charging only 1 percent more. In fact, the HOLC ultimately did operate at a loss while charging 5 percent on the loans, even though once the federal government guaranteed the principal and interest on bonds, it could issue bonds at 3 percent in 1934 and faced even lower interest costs later.

A private bad bank could not have subsidized the borrower's interest rate as the HOLC did. If the risk premium of 2 percent is added to the HOLC bond's 3 percent risk-free rate, the interest rates on private bad bank bonds likely would have been 5 percent in 1934. If it needed a 2 percent margin to make a profit, it would have had to charge 7 percent on the loans. As a result, it likely would have kept the same interest rates of between 6 and 8 percent that were on the original loans.

All of this presumes that the private bad bank could do as well as the HOLC did in identifying the loans to be purchased. If they did a worse job and the probabilities of foreclosure on the loans it purchased ranged above 30 percent, then it is not clear that the bad bank could have been a successful operation. The interest rates demanded by investors on the private bad bank bonds might have risen to levels where the bad bank could not have been viable while modifying the loans, even at the original interest rates.

A final issue is whether the HOLC crowded out private mortgage lenders, not just in the form of a private bad bank like the HOLC, but also in the form of conventional lending. There are two possible ways that this could have happened theoretically, but both seem unlikely. First, the HOLC could have taken loan customers that private lenders would have served. Since the HOLC refinanced only existing loans, it is clear that the HOLC did not compete with private lenders for new loans. As for the loans the HOLC did refinance, this is a question of whether lenders would have been willing to hang on to those customers, and empirically they preferred selling the loans to the HOLC. Second, the HOLC could have taken funding that lenders would have used to finance loans. This too seems unlikely, since the HOLC did not take deposits or otherwise compete for the savings of households. Rather, the HOLC funded itself on the bond market, where no lenders were getting funds.

# CHAPTER 6

# AN HOLC PRIMER

---

From 1933 to 1936, the HOLC purchased 1,017,821 distressed home mortgage loans from private lenders, wrote new loans for the borrowers, and then held and serviced the loans. At the time, its loan portfolio accounted for roughly one-fifth of all outstanding residential mortgages on one- to four-family, nonfarm, owner-occupied homes.[1] The HOLC received an even larger number of applications, 1,885,356, and thus accepted only 54 percent of its applications. In dollar terms, the HOLC's loan portfolio equaled $3.1 billion by 1936, which made it by far the largest single residential mortgage lender in the nation. Today a refinance program that accounted for the same share of mortgage loans would restructure 7.6 million loans worth roughly $2 trillion, or about 15 percent of gross domestic product.[2]

The HOLC was popular among both lenders and home owners. It was popular with lenders because it purchased their troubled loans at close to the full value they were owed. By doing so the HOLC restored the financial health and capacity of many mortgage lenders and assisted the liquidation of many more that failed. For home owners, the HOLC provided the opportunity to avoid foreclosure by refinancing their old loans at below-market interest rates and with repayment terms that borrowers were more able to meet. It then serviced these loans generously by making foreclosure a last resort if borrowers ended up in trouble again. Nevertheless, while the HOLC saved many of its borrowers from foreclosure, it was not able to save them all. Ultimately, the HOLC had to foreclose on nearly 20 percent of its own loans.

According to our analysis, the relief that the HOLC provided to borrowers and lenders repaired some of the deterioration in the mortgage market, reduced severe downward pressures in housing prices, and prevented some loss of home ownership in local housing markets throughout the United States. In the process, the HOLC imposed a small cost on US taxpayers through the Treasury's investment in HOLC operations. We also estimate that the government, by guaranteeing HOLC bonds and therefore assuming the risk of the operation, provided a subsidy to housing markets that was likely around 12 percent of the value of the loans it made.

In many ways, the creation, operation, and winding down of the HOLC were as impressive as its economic accomplishments. Within one and a half years, HOLC officials created a corporation with a staff of twenty thousand operating out of more than four hundred offices around the country. By then the agency had also developed the capacity to appraise homes and to record legal documents in every county in the United States. Unlike many federal government entities that persist longer and operate with a broader focus than originally intended, the HOLC stopped making loans in June 1936, as specified in the original act.[3] As the loans were repaid, the corporation reduced its size accordingly. When the last loan was repaid in 1951, the HOLC shut down.

## How the HOLC Operated

The HOLC's basic structure involved the purchase of mortgage loans from private lenders, followed by the issuance of new modified loans to the borrowers.[4] This approach actually combined two programs under one roof. The first was a "bad bank" that bought troubled assets from residential mortgage lenders, and the second was a refinance program for residential mortgage borrowers. To the extent that the HOLC is still discussed today, attention has largely been drawn to its refinance program. Nevertheless, the bad bank aspects of the HOLC would have constituted a large policy intervention even if it had not refinanced the mortgage loans that it purchased.[5]

BENEFITS TO BORROWERS

The first, and most important, benefit that borrowers received from the HOLC was simply the offer of a mortgage loan. The HOLC was the last option for borrowers who had failed to find refinancing in the private market and who

**Box 6.1. Terms of HOLC Loans**

Interest rate

    5 percent (reduced to 4.5 percent in 1939)

Length

    15 years (option for extension to up to 25 years in 1939)

Payment plan

    Choice of

      • equal payments over 15 years, or

      • interest payments only until June 1936,

        then higher payments over remainder of 15 years

Maximum loan-to-appraisal ratio

    80 percent

were likely, as a result, to end up in foreclosure. The specific terms on the HOLC loans were also beneficial and designed to help borrowers avoid re-default. Some borrowers received debt reductions, but they all benefited from other changes in contract terms. The terms of HOLC loans are outlined in box 6.1. For such risky loans, the interest rate of 5 percent was generous, as interest rates on prime private-sector home loans ranged from 6 to 8 percent across most of the country at the time. The 80 percent loan-to-value ratio was also much higher than the loan-to-value ratios in the private market, allowing some borrowers to avoid the need to carry two loans on their property. The HOLC also adopted a fifteen-year amortized loan with equal payments over the life of the loan that directly reduced the principal debt with each payment, a contractual form that was still relatively unusual at the time. Finally, in recognition of temporary underemployment due to the Depression, many borrowers were allowed to start out by paying only interest until June 1936 and then switching to higher payments over the remaining twelve years of their loans.

The initial forbearance period until June 1936 was a feature that, in other circumstances, might have been considered predatory, as it created a large increase in monthly payments after several months. For example, loans with such provisions were widely criticized in the aftermath of the mortgage crisis in the early 2000s. However, context is important. If a borrower's income is expected to improve over the first few years of a loan, then adapting the payment schedule to fit the path of expected income has sound economic reasoning, and certainly the HOLC's designers hoped and expected that its borrowers' incomes would rise by late 1936. Nevertheless, the HOLC faced a major problem with delinquencies in the late 1930s, given persistent weakness in borrowers' employment prospects and in the housing market. To address these problems, further relief was enacted in 1939 under the Mead-Barry Act, which allowed the HOLC to cut interest rates and extend loans for longer periods, as detailed in box 6.1. These additional concessions to borrowers may have been as important as any other action in helping many HOLC borrowers avoid default.

### HOME-OWNER ELIGIBILITY

Borrowers had to meet a series of criteria to be eligible for HOLC aid. Each had to live on the property on which a mortgage debt was owed. The property could not be a farm, because the government had a separate refinance program for farm mortgage loans. The property could also not be used for business purposes more than incidentally, which ruled out applications from proprietors of small businesses, like store owners, bakers, or cobblers who lived in apartments above their places of business. Properties were also not eligible if they were a part of structures that contained more than four units, eliminating owners of apartments in large apartment buildings. In addition, properties valued at over $20,000 by the HOLC appraisal could not be included. Based on housing values reported in the 1930 census, the value limit ruled out only about 3 to 4 percent of the owned nonfarm homes across the country. In New York City, with more expensive properties values, this was a larger issue, as about 10 to 11 percent of the city's properties exceeded the $20,000 limit.[6]

In a report to Congress, HOLC director W. F. Stevenson stated that the HOLC was created "for the purpose of saving the home of home owners where they are unable to secure money to pay mortgages otherwise and where the mortgagee is threatening foreclosure." The ranks of defaulted borrowers looking for such refinancing in 1933 were swelled by the Depression and by foreclosure moratoria enacted by many states beginning in early 1933 and voluntarily by some lenders as well. To be eligible, borrowers originally were required to have a distressed mortgage as of June 13, 1933, when the HOLC was established. In an amendment on April 27, 1934, these restrictions were tightened to require that the applicants had also been in default and unable to repay their loan as of June 13, 1933, but allowed those defaulting later to also apply if the default was due to "unemployment or to economic conditions or misfortune beyond the control of the applicant." The HOLC also had the authority to assist foreclosed borrowers, up to two years after they had lost title to their property. In such cases the HOLC negotiated with the new title holder—often the lender, but in some cases, a completely new owner—to buy the property itself.[7]

In order to make a final determination of an application's eligibility, the HOLC contacted the appropriate lender or lenders for documentation of outstanding debts, local governments for confirmation of any owed taxes, and credit agencies for character reports on the borrowers. Ultimately, if eligibility criteria were met and the borrower was considered a good credit risk, the HOLC would appraise the property and offer the lender a price depending on the appraisal outcome. At this point the lender would decide whether to accept.

When purchasing and refinancing loans, the HOLC had one more constraint. The principal on a restructured loan could not be more than 80 percent of a property's appraised value. In practice this proved to be an important limitation. To induce lenders to sell their loans in a typical case the HOLC paid a price that covered the principal on the loan, back taxes paid by the lender, and all or most of the interest owed on the loan. Any other back taxes were also wrapped into the loan's principal so that these could be paid directly to local authorities. In at least a third of the cases, the HOLC also provided funds to make repairs to the property. By funding tax payments and repairs, the HOLC protected itself against losses from potential foreclosure. Lending against a property with unresolved tax debt would have left the HOLC vulnerable to losing its claim if a local government foreclosed for nonpayment of taxes. Likewise, lending against a property with a bad roof or structural damage would have left the HOLC with collateral that had declined substantially in value if foreclosure became necessary.

If all of these expenses added up to more than 80 percent of the appraisal, the HOLC could ask lenders to effectively forgive some of the debt. If they did not agree, the HOLC either had to deny the application or forgive some of the debt itself by purchasing the loan at a loss. HOLC officials were not willing to take immediate losses of this sort, and so negotiation over debt forgiveness by lenders was a key part of the application process for many loans. Negotiations with lenders therefore were often difficult and heavily influenced by the HOLC's appraisal of the value of the home. However, the HOLC often weakened the impact of the 80 percent limit by appraising the home values at "normal" prices rather than the much lower Depression values. In some cases, negotiations were further complicated because the lender itself had failed; in these cases, HOLC officials were required to negotiate not only within limits set by its own authorizing legislation, but also subject to the policies set by state regulators, court-appointed receivers, or other liquidating agents.

Borrowers did not need their lenders' permission to apply, but many obtained the application forms from their lenders and likely received substantial help from them as well. Ultimately, a lender's attitude was important because the lender had to be willing to sell the loan to the HOLC at the price offered.

A successful application concluded with the HOLC disbursing any necessary payments to lenders, tax authorities, and contractors. The HOLC then treated the amount disbursed as the principal on a restructured loan, and the borrower made payments on the loan directly to the HOLC.

DEALING WITH LENDERS

Lenders benefited from the HOLC because it bought their troubled mortgage assets, using HOLC bonds as the means of payment. These bonds were better-quality assets than defaulted mortgage loans, and especially attractive to lenders once the federal government fully guaranteed them in April 1934. The bonds were transferable, so lenders could either hold on to them as investments or sell them into the secondary market to raise cash. While lenders earned interest rates of only 3 to 4 percent on HOLC bonds, this yield was doubtlessly higher than the return on defaulted mortgage loans.

In more than half the cases, lenders received HOLC bonds in amounts that fully covered the principal owed, missed interest payments, and the lenders' payments for taxes and insurance. In the rest of the cases, some amount of voluntary debt forgiveness by lenders was involved, particularly second-lien holders, although often the amounts forgiven were small and involved accrued interest rather than principal debt.[8]

Purchases by the HOLC touched all major lending groups. It purchased around 17 percent of the mortgage loans held in 1933 by the three largest groups of residential mortgage lenders—B&Ls, mutual savings banks, and individual investors. The HOLC also purchased nearly 10 percent of the home mortgages held by life insurance companies and fully 28 percent of the loans held by commercial banks.[9] Private lenders had decreased their holdings of residential mortgage debt by 15 percent ($2.7 billion) as the crisis took hold between 1930 and 1933, and then by another 15 percent ($2.6 billion) percent by 1936.[10] In the latter period the decline in private lending was almost completely offset by increases in the HOLC's mortgage loan holdings.

The separation of troubled assets into a separate institution is the defining feature of a bad bank. A key purpose of a bad bank like the HOLC is to allow existing lenders to reduce the uncertainty associated with having troubled assets on their books. In addition, a bad bank can use economies of scale to assemble a specialized staff dedicated to resolving troubled assets in a way that may be infeasible for individual institutions. This segregation strategy has been used in a wide variety of circumstances throughout history, including the 1930s, sometimes by individual institutions splitting themselves in two, and other times by groups of institutions collecting their assets in single entities. In any case, the main challenge of a bad bank is finding people willing to invest in it, a problem solved in the case of the HOLC by the issuance of government-guaranteed bonds.[11]

The bad bank characterization may seem less apt in cases where the HOLC bought loans from failed lenders, which accounted for about 13 percent of HOLC loans. In these cases the eligibility requirements and the application process worked a bit differently. With such institutions, the HOLC did not limit its asset purchases to only distressed loans. It purchased any mortgage the institutions were willing to sell, in an effort to improve the cash position of the institutions. Closed lenders were likely to seek liquidation of any assets they could, even nondistressed mortgage loans, and so the HOLC was able to act differently, since it was not subject to the sorts of short-term pressures that mortgage lenders faced in the mid-1930s. Failed lenders were usually not struggling to fence off viable parts of their operations and put their losses behind them, but viability was not always a lost cause, and HOLC officials believed that it could help these lenders reopen. Even if the HOLC purchases did not help the institutions reopen, the HOLC at least helped them to pay off their depositors and thus to provide those depositors with access to their badly needed savings. In this way the HOLC demonstrated that a central function of a bad bank was not just to save private lending institutions but also to repair the broader damage caused by the toxic assets these institutions held on their books.

### HOW THE HOLC FUNDED ITS ACTIVITIES

To support its outlays—to lenders, tax authorities, and contractors and for administrative expenses—the HOLC had two funding sources. The first was a capital investment of $200 million by the US Treasury. While this was not an insubstantial amount of money, it was not nearly enough to cover the $3 billion in loans for which the HOLC eventually required funding. It was quite useful, however, in giving the HOLC an immediate infusion of cash to establish operations. The bulk of the HOLC's funds instead came from bonds that it issued both on the open market and to specific lenders in exchange for their mortgages.

Before April 1934, the federal government guaranteed only the interest on HOLC bonds, and so encountered some difficulty in persuading lenders to accept its bonds in exchange for their loans. All things considered, the lenders naturally would have preferred cash. If a lender refused to take bonds, the HOLC would consider exchanging cash for the loan but only if the mortgage, taxes, and other debts were not in excess of 40 percent of the value of the property, a much more stringent limit than the 80 percent used for deals financed with bonds.[12] Table 7.1 (see p. 73) indicates that as many as 7.7 percent of applications failed because lenders refused to accept bonds. That figure is likely a bit overstated, though, because the figures cover a period at the beginning of the program's operations when the bond problems were more salient. The concern was large enough, however, that HOLC officials asked Congress for the guarantee, and Roosevelt, following his strong political instincts, framed the issue as a "moral obligation" required of a Congress that wanted to see that the program succeeded.[13]

During testimony regarding the bill that guaranteed these bonds, the chairman of the House Committee on Banking and Currency stated that "[e]xperience has shown that there is great difficulty in persuading mortgagees [i.e., lenders] to accept these bonds even at the present rate. We had to resort to this method of securing the principal, or having the Government secure the principal, in order to make the law effective."[14] Figure 6.1 shows how the prices of HOLC bonds improved significantly in January 1934, when Roosevelt first proposed their guarantee, and finally traded at par value in April 1934, when the guarantee was enacted. While the guarantee was not proposed until the

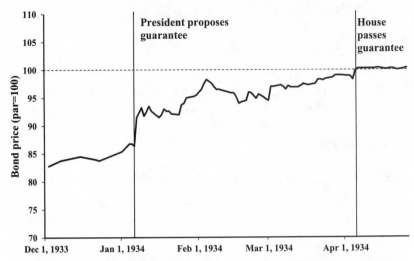

**Figure 6.1.** *HOLC bond prices. These are the bid prices on the first series of HOLC bonds with maturity in July 1951, and a 4 percent interest rate. (Data from the financial pages of the* New York Times.*)*

program was about six months old in January 1934, it improved the reception of the HOLC's bonds immediately, and most of the HOLC's refinancing had not yet been completed. After the guarantee, there is little in the historical record to indicate lenders were still concerned about the quality of the bonds.[15]

The guarantee of bonds had important implications for whose money was at stake. Without a guarantee, bondholders were initially left to bear the risk on whether the entire principal would be redeemed at maturity, a risk that depended on whether borrowers were able to pay their loans. The guarantee made HOLC bonds as safe as Treasury securities and therefore as good as cash to lenders, which is what they really wanted. For the HOLC's finances, the guarantee lowered their interest costs of issuing bonds, since those receiving the bonds did not demand as large an interest rate to compensate them for risk. Altogether, this guarantee made it easier for the HOLC to issue bonds to lenders and to others and at a lower cost, but it also transferred all of the financial risk of the program away from lenders to taxpayers.

This brings us to a major question about HOLC finances: did the program lose money? In chapter 10, we discuss this question in more detail, along with other aspects of the HOLC's finances. The bottom line is that the HOLC probably cost taxpayers a small amount of money, but it did not cause a large loss. Popular discussions of the HOLC often note that it turned a small accounting profit, but this long-repeated claim is based on misleading figures that do not take into account all of the costs imposed on the federal government by the HOLC.

## A Chronology of HOLC Operations

SETTING UP SHOP

The Home Owners' Loan Corporation Act of June 13, 1933, created the HOLC, placed it under the jurisdiction of the Federal Home Loan Bank Board, and gave it three years to purchase and refinance distressed loans. Like many other New Deal programs, the HOLC was created, staffed, and began operations in an impressively short period of time. In its first six months the HOLC opened 50 state offices (including in Hawaii and Washington, DC) and 255 district offices and agencies, and hired nearly seven thousand employees. By its peak, just eighteen months later, the HOLC employed more than twenty thousand people. In addition, the HOLC also had to develop policies and procedures for handling more than one million applications within just its first year and then to evaluate and complete complex loan purchases and modifications.

The corporation initially focused on publicizing its mission. President Roosevelt highlighted the program in fireside chats both before and after he signed the act, and pamphlets describing the program were then circulated throughout the country. The corporation also enlisted newspapers in all major markets to carry prominent stories describing the benefits of the program to borrowers and how to apply. The publicity was so successful in New York City that 15,000 applications were received by mail before the first HOLC office there opened on August 14, 1933. On opening day officials were greeted by an additional 150 home owners lined up outside the office door to apply in person.[16] The nationwide total of HOLC applications reached 400,000 by September of that year, 700,000 by December, and then doubled again by the following June. The flow of HOLC applications over time is shown in solid bars in figure 6.2.

At first the evaluation and dispersal of loans simply could not keep up with the large number of applications. Although applicants were frustrated by the delay, some holdup was inevitable. In conducting its operations, the HOLC staff had to develop procedures for appraisals and administrative actions de-

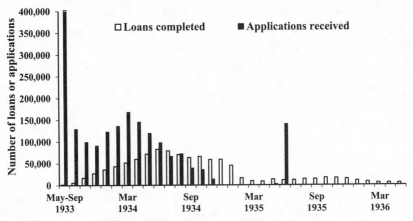

**Figure 6.2.** *HOLC applications received and loans completed by month, 1933–1936. The first observation covers the first five months of operations, as statistics were not reported separately for these months. (Data from Harriss 1951, 30.)*

signed specifically for a distressed mortgage market. The HOLC procedures then had to be tailored to conform to local market conventions, zoning restrictions, and property laws. Each home and property needed to be appraised separately to determine its state of repair and its value in a market where very few homes were selling and prices had been dropping dramatically. Each loan application had to be evaluated carefully, given that borrowers were all behind on payments and taxes. In some cases legal disputes over who held title to the property needed to be resolved. Further, the HOLC had to coordinate and negotiate with thousands of large and small lenders to prevent foreclosure while applications were being processed. The purchase of the loan also required delicate negotiations, as did the determination of whether the borrower met the definition of being in trouble "through no fault of his own."

Selecting and training employees was critical for the successful operation of a hierarchical administrative structure that handled complex property and mortgage loan transactions across thousands of local housing markets. The HOLC hired and trained managers, lawyers, paralegals, secretaries, economists, property appraisers, financial specialists, and general staff to run hundreds of offices and also decided to appoint an attorney and a local appraiser in each of the nation's three thousand counties. The hiring process involved plowing through thousands of applications, because large numbers of people were seeking work.

Not surprisingly, it took some time for this elaborate lending apparatus to catch up with a virtual avalanche of applications. In its first year, the HOLC received 80 percent of the total applications it would ultimately receive, but made only 38 percent of its eventual loan total. The initial flood of applications was so large that the HOLC operated with a six-month backlog of cases during that year. While the first loan applications were approved in the summer of 1933, it was not until March 1934 that the monthly volume of loan approvals reached fifty thousand applications, as shown in the white bars in figure 6.2.[17]

The original $2 billion limit Congress set on the HOLC's refinancing volume was increased to $3 billion in early 1934. But by fall of that year, the corporation determined that the applications in process would exhaust even the new higher limit, and so it announced in November 1934 that it would stop receiving applications. The announcement may have been partially motivated by a desire to discourage applications from less distressed borrowers. The debate in Congress certainly reflected this. After the application window had been open for a year and a half, some members of Congress argued that the nation's distressed home owners had already been given a reasonable length of time to apply. Indeed, as early as the fall of 1933, HOLC officials had begun discouraging applications from home owners who did not meet the program's eligibility requirements or who could not demonstrate sufficient distress. As HOLC officials often stated, their agency was not in a position to refinance every home mortgage in America, nor did they have a mandate to do so.[18]

Despite these objections and observations, the cap on the issuance of bonds was raised again in May 1935 to $4.75 billion, and an additional 145,000 applications were received in a brief window during late May and June 1935. The number of loans processed after this surge of applications, shown in figure 6.2, was relatively small, however, and the total value of loans restructured did not rise much beyond $3 billion.

## DEALING WITH FORECLOSURES

As set in the enabling legislation, the HOLC permanently ceased refinancing loans on June 12, 1936. From that point until the liquidation of the last loan in April 1951, the HOLC was devoted primarily to servicing its existing loans.

The largest problem that the HOLC faced after completing the loan restructurings was dealing with the properties of home owners who could not repay their new loans. Ultimately, the HOLC refinancing could not prevent the loss of homes for 198,141 of its borrowers (19.4 percent). Despite many attempts to help delinquent home owners find jobs and means of repayment, many fell behind on the HOLC loan payments for a year or more, and the HOLC eventually foreclosed. While this is a large rate of foreclosure, it is important to keep in mind that most of these mortgages likely would have ended in foreclosure had they not been refinanced by the HOLC. Nevertheless, the politics of a corporation backed by the federal government foreclosing on its own citizens were tricky. One can only imagine the anger directed toward a government-backed entity that would evict its citizens from their homes. Of course, if the HOLC had ruled out the possibility of foreclosure, it would have grossly distorted the incentives of its borrowers. Without any fear that they would be evicted, there would have been little reason for them to bother paying back their mortgages.

Most of the foreclosures took place before 1941. While the employment prospects of HOLC borrowers were generally recovering after 1933, the unemployment rate was still 14 percent in 1937, and an economic setback in 1938 caused it to rise again to 19 percent. The number of foreclosures surged in fiscal years 1937 and 1938 because the forbearance period on principal payments ended in June 1936, resulting in higher monthly payments. The goal of that forbearance period had been to give borrowers enough time to find a steady income, but a number of borrowers were still struggling to find work in late 1936 and soon fell behind when their monthly payment plans required higher payments. The main wave of HOLC foreclosures then followed. Since many of the borrowers had been delinquent for more than two years on their original loans and were now delinquent on the HOLC restructured loan, they likely had not made any substantial payments on their homes for half a decade. This wave of foreclosures was reduced by two forces. First, the liberalizations of the 1939 Mead-Barry Act lowered the monthly payments required of borrowers. Second, the economic expansion of the early 1940s helped to buoy the incomes and house values of borrowers who had avoided foreclosure up to that point.

Once the HOLC foreclosed on the properties, it worked to figure out how to dispose of them. Most of the properties had fallen into various stages of disrepair after the home owners had stopped making payments. To make the homes more attractive for resale, the HOLC refurbished them and then had to determine the best time to resell them. HOLC officials were well aware of the continued decline in housing values in the latter half of the 1930s and worried that a flood of sales of foreclosed housing would further damage property values in the short run. In consequence, they often rented out the homes for a period of time and spread home sales over a longer time frame to try to avoid driving prices down. As seen in figure 6.3, the peak year for HOLC property sales was the fiscal year 1940, two years after the peak in acquisitions. By that time the unemployment rate had fallen from 19 percent in 1938 to 14 percent. The remaining sales occurred in the 1940s as unemployment rates continued to drop. During the war, demand for existing homes grew, as new house

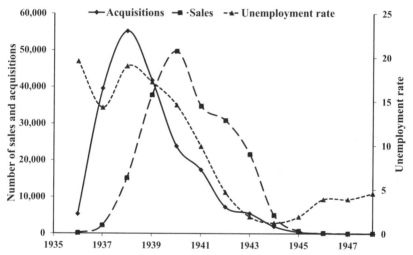

**Figure 6.3.** Unemployment rate and HOLC foreclosure acquisitions and sales, fiscal years 1934–1936 through 1948–1951. (Data from Federal Home Loan Bank Administration 1952, 26.) The totals for 1936 cover all acquisitions and sales from 1934 to 1936. The totals for 1948 include all activity from 1948 through 1951. Unemployment rate is calculated by Stanley Lebergott, series D-85 in US Bureau of the Census (1975, 135), and considers people on work relief as unemployed. The unemployment rate for 1936 is the average for 1934–1936, and for 1948 is the average for 1948–1951.

construction was limited, and families had spare money because consumer goods were rationed while incomes rose.

WINDING DOWN

The HOLC was an emergency program that Congress intended and designed to shut down after its purpose was achieved. The HOLC's enabling legislation contained important provisions that prevented the HOLC from becoming a permanent source of federally subsidized home mortgage financing. HOLC lending was restricted to the three-year period starting in June 1933 and was limited in total dollar volume. The HOLC was also required to retire its outstanding bonds with the mortgage principal repayments it received rather than using the funds to finance additional activities. The shuttering of the HOLC was a relatively rare act for a federal government entity. Many government agencies and corporations have hung on by switching emphasis to other activities loosely related to their original missions.

Throughout its life the HOLC stayed primarily focused on its original mortgage refinance mission, though the initial HOLC Act allowed for some longer-term investments. These other investments included a requirement that the HOLC provide the initial capitalization for the Federal Savings and Loan Insurance Corporation, and an authorization to invest in the stock of new federally chartered savings and loans associations in areas not well served by existing associations. During World War II, the HOLC was also used by the National Housing Agency to convert and manage properties as housing for war workers at a direct cost of roughly $80 million.

In 1940 when unemployment rates were still nearly 10 percent, the HOLC still serviced 850,000 active loans. But by then it did not need the large staff that had been required to process applications and make loans. As a result, its staff fell below ten thousand, spread across only ninety-eight offices. During the war years, the HOLC's borrowers began to pay off their loans as they moved to new houses or as their incomes improved. At the end of World War II in 1945, only about 530,000 loans were being serviced by two thousand HOLC employees in thirteen offices. By 1947 roughly one thousand employees in three offices handled the remaining 320,000 loans.[19] Figure 6.4 shows the winding down of HOLC activities, as most of the foreclosed property had been sold off by the mid-1940s and outstanding loans dropped significantly.

By the late 1940s liquidation became the highest priority. It was uneco-

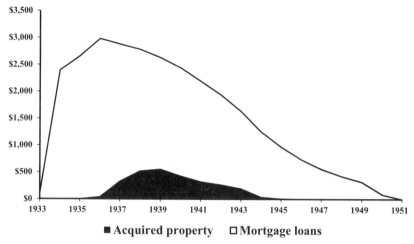

■ **Acquired property**   □ **Mortgage loans**

**Figure 6.4.** *Value of HOLC loans and owned properties, 1933–1951. Dollar figures are in millions, on December 31 from 1933 to 1935, and on June 30 from 1936 to 1951. (Data from the HOLC's annual reports.) Loans include both the original loans from 1933 to 1936 and new loans originated after 1936 to the buyers of the HOLC's owned properties.*

nomical for the HOLC to service a continually shrinking number of loans, with borrowers scattered all across the country. Moreover, the HOLC's support for the housing market was no longer a pressing need. Private lenders were happy to deal with the HOLC's extant borrowers, who had been dutifully paying their mortgages for over a decade. As a result, the HOLC encouraged its borrowers to pay in full or to refinance with private lenders. Eventually, it sold off its remaining mortgages in bulk by local markets within each state. By April 1951, HOLC operations were effectively over.

# CHAPTER 7

# THE LENDERS'
# GOOD DEAL

---

Most discussions of the HOLC focus on the relief given to borrowers. The HOLC itself always emphasized the borrowers' side of the program in public and in its annual reports. The name, the *Home Owners' Loan Corporation*, was meant to reinforce that mandate to focus on the home owners. Yet aid to lenders was a major part of the program. For every borrower whose debt was refinanced by the HOLC, there was at least one lender who voluntarily sold its loan to the HOLC. Thus, the HOLC was much more than a mortgage refinance program. It also served as a "bad bank." The HOLC purchased nonperforming loans from lenders by exchanging them for HOLC bonds that were guaranteed by the federal government. The lenders were therefore able to replace the nonperforming loans on their books with risk-free bonds that could be readily sold. Essentially, the lenders were able to dump their "toxic assets" on the HOLC, putting them in better positions to make new loans.

The key to success in reaching borrowers was getting lenders to sell their troubled loans. If the HOLC had demanded that the lenders take a "haircut" by offering only 50 cents per dollar of the debts owed by borrowers, lenders likely would have balked. In that scenario, with few loan purchases the HOLC would have been unable to reach those borrowers who were in trouble "through no fault of their own." To achieve a large size, the HOLC had to offer terms that lenders would accept.

Of course, lenders did have some interest in selling these nonperforming assets. On the typical loan sold to the HOLC, borrowers were in arrears on principal for over two years, and lenders had often made some tax and insurance payments to allow the borrowers to stay in their homes. If a lender refused an HOLC offer and held on to its loan, foreclosure was likely the next move. Foreclosure was and still is a long and uncertain process during which the lender would have to pay taxes and cover maintenance costs for the property. In many states, the process was slowed further by mortgage moratoria laws enacted to delay foreclosures. As some offsetting compensation, the lender might have been able to rent the home for some rental income. When trying to sell the property, the lender faced a deeply depressed real estate market; therefore, the sale price likely would not cover the full debt that was owed.

Lenders were more likely to accept HOLC offers the closer those offers came to covering the accumulated debts owed by the borrowers. Giving lenders a good deal was not without a cost, however, as any additional dollar spent in purchasing loans from lenders was a dollar that the HOLC tried to recoup from borrowers. The bargaining process with lenders became somewhat of a balancing act between the relief provided to lenders and to borrowers.

In the final analysis, the lenders did well in their negotiations with the HOLC. In one sample of HOLC loans from New York, New Jersey, and Connecticut, slightly over half of the lenders received an amount in HOLC bonds equal to all that they were owed, including the principal on the loan, the taxes and insurance they had paid, and the unpaid interest on the loan. This was likely a substantial improvement compared to their situation if they had foreclosed on the house and sold it in 1933 when market values had fallen 20 to 40 percent. Before 1930 first mortgage loans were generally written for less than two-thirds of the appraised home value, so lenders might have recovered the principal on the original loan through foreclosure, though at a delay. They might not have gotten back much unpaid interest, taxes, or insurance. In these cases a lender could have sued for a deficiency judgment against the borrower. But by 1933 court cases and legislation had curtailed the use of deficiency judgments in many states. Even where they had not, a suit against most borrowers would have cost a great deal in legal fees with little chance of recovering money from people who had likely lost their jobs or had some other disaster befall them.

### The Need to Encourage Lender Participation

Officially, borrowers were the ones who made applications to the HOLC for their loans to be refinanced. However, an application was successful only if the HOLC was able to buy the loan from the lender. The sale of the loan was a voluntary transaction because the HOLC could not force the lender to participate. Each borrower had signed a mortgage contract with his or her lender, and the Constitution generally prevents governmental infringement on private contracts at will. This is a key constraint on any program that is designed to modify or refinance mortgage loans. In fact, winning the participation of lenders has been a central issue in modern mortgage modification programs, as the modern programs have struggled to give lenders enough incentive to voluntarily put modifications in place. Understanding how the HOLC won the participation of lenders is central to understanding how the HOLC refinanced as many loans as it did.

The HOLC knew that lenders were willing to turn down their offers if the lenders found those offers to be inadequate. HOLC officials in Michigan noted that in their dealings with Prudential Insurance, for example, the insurance company would "accept no losses. In rare exceptions, they will accept an amount equal to their capital investment."[1] In another case a home owner and mortgage borrower in Hartford, Connecticut, believed his property to be worth $5,000, but an HOLC appraisal estimated the value to be only $3,420. Meanwhile, the borrower owed $3,755 to the lender for the principal of the loan and unpaid interest payments, and $175 to the local government for back taxes. After following its procedures, the HOLC offered at most $2,500. The lender's lowest offer was to reduce their claim to $3,000. Neither the lender nor the HOLC would bridge that gap, and the application never succeeded.[2]

Lenders who held first mortgages could rationalize their reluctance to accept losses in their negotiations with the HOLC. Traditional underwriting standards during the 1920s typically set maximum loan size at 50–60 percent of the home's value, and many lenders imposed even more conservative standards. These relatively low loan-to-value ratios were set so that lenders would be assured of recovering their investments even if property values fell dramatically, as they did in the early 1930s. Although borrowers used second mortgages to increase the share of the home value that they borrowed, first mortgage lenders had reason to claim that they, just like borrowers, held distressed loans because of broad market forces rather than their own lax underwriting standards. Against this backdrop, lenders might have felt it was prudent to foreclose on their homes and wait patiently for the housing market to improve rather than take an immediate loss by selling to the HOLC.

**Table 7.1. Reasons that HOLC applications were rejected or withdrawn**

| Reason for rejection or incompletion | Number | % |
|---|---|---|
| Inadequate security | 103,145 | 17.9 |
| Lack of distress | 72,778 | 12.6 |
| Failure of applicant to cooperate | 56,186 | 9.7 |
| Property of nonhomestead type | 46,353 | 8.0 |
| Mortgagee's refusal to accept bonds | 44,446 | 7.7 |
| Unstable credit or income of mortgagor | 43,249 | 7.5 |
| Property primarily for commercial use | 27,668 | 4.8 |
| Defective or insufficient title | 20,362 | 3.5 |
| Miscellaneous | 73,361 | 12.7 |
| Application withdrawn | 90,094 | 15.6 |
| Total | 577,642 | 100.0 |

*Source*: Harriss 1951, 24.

How often did the lenders and the HOLC fail to come to agreement? The only systematic evidence available comes from an internal HOLC study of the first 577,642 applications that were either rejected by the HOLC or withdrawn, about two-thirds of failed applications over the life of the program. Of the reasons listed in table 7.1 for the lack of success, 17.9 percent failed due to "inadequate security," which indicated that the value of the house (i.e., the security) was not large enough for the HOLC to make an offer that the lender would accept.

Another 7.7 percent were not completed because the lender refused to accept HOLC bonds. The refusals likely occurred before April 1934 when the federal government was guaranteeing only the interest and not the principal on HOLC bonds. After the government fully guaranteed the bonds, it is unlikely that there were many refusals, and the unwillingness to accept bonds as indicated in table 7.1 may have been just another way to say that no deal was struck. There were enough refusals at first, though, to indicate that lender participation was a real concern.

The guarantee of the bonds was itself a major concession to lenders, and in a very meaningful way it transferred the risks of the program from the lenders to the taxpayers. When the bonds were not fully guaranteed, lenders bore the risk. In such a structure, lenders would bet that their distressed and non-refinanced mortgages were worth less than HOLC bonds that were backed by a large pool of mortgages restructured by the HOLC. Evidently, lenders and bond market participants had significant doubts. Ultimately, the transfer of this risk to taxpayers was a large effective subsidy to lenders.

## How the HOLC Achieved Lender Participation

The HOLC was able to reach such a large size because it made lenders offers that were attractive enough to convince them to participate. Part of the attractiveness came from the guarantee of the bonds given to the lenders, but the attractiveness was also in large part due to the generous values of bonds the HOLC offered, relative to the debts owed to the lenders. In other words, the HOLC was able to make offers with values greater than the lenders would realize by refusing the HOLC's offer and likely having to foreclose.

When the HOLC bought a loan, it had the capacity to offer any price that it liked. However, the law creating the corporation capped the value of a new HOLC loan at 80 percent of the appraised value of the property. Therefore, the HOLC had a choice. If the HOLC paid a lender more than 80 percent of the property's appraisal value, it would have automatically created a loss for itself on the purchase of the loan, since it could not ask the borrower to pay back that large an amount. Of course, taking a loss is something they could have decided to do in the name of relief, but HOLC officials ruled out such a strategy in practice. Consequently, the appraisal was central to determining the maximum payment available to the lender, which in turn was the main determinant of lender participation. Fundamentally, the HOLC gave lenders a good deal. It did this by implementing a generous appraisal strategy, which raised the cap on maximum allowable payments to lenders.

The importance of appraisals is illustrated by the example of Julia Carter, whose debt to the New Michigan Building and Loan Association totaled $3,700. This was a promising case for the HOLC. Internal correspondence noted that "the New Michigan B&L is not very anxious to take this piece of property back as they would have to spend about $1500 in taxes and repairs before the place could be rented."[3] Foreclosure would just have allowed New Michigan to rent the property and perhaps generate some revenue before trying to sell it in a bad market.

New Michigan bargained with the HOLC over the extent of the write-down of the debt. HOLC internal memos document the HOLC's attempt to pay the B&L as much as they could:

We have had the appraisal reviewed to determine whether or not it could be raised to take care of the various obligations which the property is encumbered with. Everybody agrees that the appraisal is, at the present time, as high as it can possibly be. Of course, you know, under the law, we are not allowed to loan over 80% of the appraisal amount. Therefore it would be impossible to increase the amount of the offer. The offer may appear to be low, but this is because no taxes have been paid since 1928 and the house is in need of some repairs.[4]

The important part of this quote is how it describes officials trying to raise the appraisal as high as they could get it, in order to pay lenders high prices. The HOLC's appraisals were generous in the sense that they were on average significantly above the HOLC's own estimates of the prices at which the properties would have sold in the depressed markets in the mid-1930s.

To see the importance of the distinction between appraisals and market values, consider the example we construct in table 7.2. Imagine a home that was purchased in 1929 for $2,000, with a loan of $1,000. By 1934 the market price of the home had fallen 40 percent to $1,200. The borrower also owed

**Table 7.2. An example of how appraisal methods affected the HOLC's maximum loan amounts**

| | |
|---|---|
| Original purchase price in 1929 | $2,000 |
| Price estimates in 1934 | |
|     Market price in 1934 | $1,200 |
|     Long-run appraised value in 1934 | $1,500 |
| Debts owed in 1934 | |
|     Original principal on loan | $1,000 |
|     Missed interest payments and taxes | $200 |
|       Total | $1,200 |
| Loan limits from different appraisal methods | |
|     80 percent limit with 1934 market price of $1,200 | $960 |
|     80 percent limit with long run appraised value of $1,500 | $1,200 |

$1,200 to the lender because he had missed $200 in interest and tax payments and still owed the original $1,000 in principal. Had the HOLC appraised the home at its 1934 market price of $1,200, the rule limiting the loan to no more than 80 percent of the appraisal would have meant that the most the HOLC could offer to refinance was $960. If the HOLC offered the lender $960 in bonds for the loan debt of $1,200, the lender would have needed to decide whether it was worth giving up $240 out of the debt owed to transfer the loan to the HOLC. Most lenders were not willing to accept a deal in which they would take a haircut of $240, or 20 percent of the debt owed.

The logic of the 80 percent limit provides an easy source of inference when thinking about individual cases. As an example, the first deal struck in New York State was relatively straightforward.[5] The Rachlin family from the Bensonhurst neighborhood of Brooklyn, New York, had fallen behind on their payments after Mr. Rachlin lost his job in October 1931. At the time the loan was purchased, the Rachlins owed $8,400 to their lender on a house with an appraised value of $13,500. The newspaper article describing the Rachlins' situation did not discuss the terms of the HOLC transaction, but we can make some educated guesses. The HOLC likely bought the loan for the full $8,400 owed, and the lender likely took no loss, given that the 80 percent loan-to-appraisal ratio was not exceeded. Since the Rachlins owed another $300 to New York City tax authorities, the HOLC's restructured loan for the Rachlins entailed a slightly higher principal debt of about $8,700. Potentially the loan could have been larger had the HOLC determined that some emergency repairs were needed to preserve the property and protect the value of the loan collateral.

In making appraisals HOLC officials often stated that they were taking a long-run view of the value of the home.[6] Since home prices had fallen by 20 to 50 percent between 1930 and 1934 in most parts of the country, a long-run view of home values gave the HOLC substantial leeway in setting an appraisal value that was substantially higher than the 1934–1935 market prices of the homes. By picking an appraisal value of $1,500, partway between the prices of $2,000 in 1929 and $1,200 in 1934, the HOLC could purchase the $1,200 debt for the full value from the lender and then refinance the full $1,200 owed by the borrower.[7]

To increase its ability to accommodate lenders, the HOLC raised many of its appraisals in this fashion. A sample of HOLC loans from New York, New

Jersey, and Connecticut provides the only evidence currently available that allows comparisons of the HOLC appraisals to their estimates of mid-1930s market prices for the same properties. For the properties in the sample, the final appraisal exceeded the market price estimate in 58.5 percent of the observations, equaled it in 10.6 percent, and was lower in 30.9 percent. Across all observations, the average markup was 4.2 percent. For properties on which the HOLC ultimately foreclosed, appraisals appear to have been raised more on average, as 76.8 percent of the HOLC's appraisals exceeded the estimated market price, and the average markup was 6.3 percent.[8]

These aggregate statistics include many cases in which borrowers had debts well below the 80 percent debt-to-appraisal limit. In such cases, it did not matter much if the appraisal was higher or lower than the market price estimates, because the HOLC was able to pay lenders and tax authorities the full amounts owed to them without violating the 80 percent debt-to-appraisal limit when writing new loans to the borrowers. In the tristate sample, the HOLC was in fact much less likely to have high appraisals (relative to market price estimates) when borrowers had low debts. In contrast, when borrowers had high debts, the HOLC was much more likely to have high appraisals, allowing them to pay higher amounts to lenders than if they had stuck to market price estimates. In this way, borrowers would be left with debts that were technically not in excess of 80 percent of appraisals, though they could be in excess of 80 percent of market price estimates.[9]

HOLC officials candidly described their desire to accommodate lenders in internal memos. For example, a March 1934 memo reviewing New Jersey lending contains a description of appraisals being manipulated in order to accommodate existing debts:

It has been the policy of the Camden Office to endeavor in every way to make appraisals that will fit the present encumbrances, in total, of the property. The Fee Appraiser, along with his order for appraisal, is given a copy of the preliminary appraisal. He is given a recapitulation sheet showing the amount due, including all existing liens, and showing the amount of appraisal that will be necessary to cover same, already imported on the recapitulation sheet. He has received specific instructions, supposed to have come from the State Appraiser, directing them that inasmuch as we are bailing out the owner, make the appraisal high enough to cover it. The District Appraiser, in case the appraisal does not fit, attempts to suggest and argue with the Fee Appraiser to raise his appraisal to fit the picture.[10]

All of these adjustments of appraisals were made possible by the fact that the bill establishing the HOLC neglected to specify an appraisal methodology. Instead it allowed the HOLC to develop and implement its own methodology. The HOLC could not loan more than 80 percent of the appraisal for any given property, but since the definition of an appraisal was up for grabs, this constraint was significantly weakened. In the process, it is not surprising to learn that lenders encouraged the HOLC to manipulate appraisals in this fashion. A letter from the HOLC's state manager of Connecticut reported the lenders' encouragements to the national office: "We are being criticized by certain lending institutions in the State of Connecticut for what they claim is a lack of proper interpretation of the spirit of the HOLC Act and we are supposed to interpret the act as allowing us to make the appraisals liberal."[11]

It is worth noting that when the HOLC bought loans for less than the full value of the debt, it did not necessarily represent real losses to lenders. Had the HOLC not come along, many lenders likely would have never received the full amount of interest that had not been paid on the loan. Further, we can find no evidence that the HOLC sought to increase its leverage by bargaining with lenders over multiple loans at once. It appears that lenders negotiated with the HOLC over each loan separately. This may have been for the sake of expediency, given that multiple loans from a single lender were unlikely to have been ready for negotiation at any given point in time. Nevertheless, it suggests that for every loan purchased from a lender, the lender expected the HOLC bonds to be a more attractive investment than the loan itself.

## How Lenders Fared

The HOLC never gave much information about its negotiations with lenders. In one of its annual reports, it estimated that across all of its loans, 7 percent of borrowers' outstanding debts were forgiven by lenders, on average.[12] Otherwise, we rely on the tristate sample for information. The sample gives a similar figure, indicating that 9 percent of borrowers' outstanding debts were forgiven by lenders. Therefore, in aggregate, lenders appear to have recouped over 90 percent of what was owed them, including principal on the loans, missed interest payments, and the lenders' payments for taxes and insurance.

In slightly more than half of the tristate sample, lenders took no losses at all, as they received HOLC bonds in amounts that fully covered all the debts owed to them. In these cases, the borrowers' debts did not exceed the 80 percent limit, and therefore HOLC officials did not even ask them to consider forgiving debt. In the rest of the cases, slightly less than half the sample, some amount of voluntary debt forgiveness by lenders was involved, particularly second-lien holders, although often the amounts forgiven were small and involved accrued interest rather than principal debt.

Perhaps the most interesting cases are those in which borrowers had two lenders and at least one of the lenders had to forgive some debt in order for the loan to be accepted because the borrowers' total outstanding debts exceeded 80 percent of the HOLC appraisal at the time of application. About 25 percent of the borrowers in the sample satisfied these criteria, owing debts this high on at least two loans. In these cases, some lender had to take a haircut, and over 95 percent of the junior lien holders indeed forgave some debt. It is natural that losses were so widespread among junior lien holders because these lenders were last in line to receive payments in a foreclosure, and, in fact, it is somewhat difficult to explain why a small number of them actually did not take losses in these cases. Half of these second-lien holders took fairly substantial cuts, receiving one-third of their claims or less. In comparison, the first-lien holders in these cases did better. Over half took no haircut at all, and three-quarters recovered at least 94 percent. Therefore, the conservative underwriting standards of the 1920s, with low loan-to-value ratios of first mortgage loans, truly did protect first mortgage lenders from losses.

Across the whole sample, only about a third of first mortgage holders forgave any debt when selling loans to the HOLC, and the average recovery among first mortgage lenders was over 96 percent. In contrast, 70 percent of second mortgage lenders forgave some debt, and their aggregate recovery rate was much lower, around 45 percent. The payments from the HOLC to junior lien holders did not always represent their entire compensation, however. The HOLC in some cases allowed an original, recalcitrant junior lien holder to create a new second mortgage, subordinate to the new HOLC mortgage. The second mortgages could not exceed 20 percent of the HOLC appraisal, so that when the second mortgage was combined with the HOLC mortgage, the total debt remained no more than 100 percent of the appraisal value. These payments underscore the main finding that the HOLC went to great lengths to offer enough to lenders to ensure that they participated in the program.[13]

The tristate sample relates to loans actually made by the HOLC and therefore does not capture applications that failed because lenders refused to forgive debt. We know that such cases existed from the examples given in this chapter, which were taken from loan files stored at the National Archives. The evidence presented in table 7.1, moreover, suggests that perhaps about 18 percent of applications failed because of those refusals. The rate of refusal was not so high, however, as to prevent the HOLC from aiding a large proportion of distressed home owners.

Finally, in considering how lenders fared, it is important to consider that lenders ended up holding bonds that paid only 3 percent interest per year and gave up loans with interest rates ranging between 6 and 8 percent per year. Lenders were willing to do so, of course, because they were likely not receiving interest payments on their loans and faced additional losses given the likelihood of foreclosure, while the low return on the HOLC bonds was guaranteed by the federal government.[14] This guarantee, together with the HOLC's appraisal methodology, created an attractive opportunity for lenders, so that the HOLC was able to refinance more than a million loans.

## Consequences for Borrowers of the Lenders' Good Deal

The HOLC's emphasis on accommodating lenders, by adopting higher appraisals that delivered higher payments to lenders, had consequences for borrowers. It constrained the HOLC's ability to offer debt reductions to borrowers when it refinanced loans. Reductions in debt were sought only for borrowers with incumbent debts that exceeded 80 percent of the appraisal. If that threshold was not reached, the HOLC required such borrowers to repay the full debt they owed the lender. Even so, the generous terms offered on the refinanced loans described in the next chapter show that the borrowers generally received a good deal as well.

The HOLC's generous approach to lenders benefited borrowers in another sense. In the HOLC's role as a bad bank, the assistance it provided lenders also helped repair the mortgage market and the housing market in general. Had the HOLC loan purchase program not been created, mortgage lenders throughout the nation likely would have been forced to resort to protracted foreclosure proceedings against hundreds of thousands of borrowers between 1933 and 1936. In doing so, lender capital and lending capacity would have been frozen for several years longer, making it difficult for potential home owners to get credit; the housing crisis would have become much more severe, and recovery postponed even longer.

# CHAPTER 8

# THE BORROWERS'
# GOOD DEAL

I am now most emphatically concerned with the fact that I am about to lose
that which is most dear to me—MY HOME. This house is solid brick, ten rooms, hot
water heat, slate roof, and although I built it twenty four years ago, it is still in
excellent condition, for I have always taken good care of it, and it is well worth
saving.
— HOLC applicant Anna Cobb, writing to Eleanor Roosevelt, October 28, 1935

Anna Cobb, quoted above, expressed despair at losing her house, a possession
that was "most dear" to her.[1] Her lender, the First National Bank of Detroit,
had failed, and she wrote Eleanor Roosevelt in a final but unlikely attempt to
get her debts refinanced with the HOLC after her application was rejected. In
the early 1930s, Anna's family was one of about five million nonfarm households in the United States that owed mortgage debts on their homes, and the
HOLC refinanced roughly 20 percent of those between late 1933 and 1936.
By 1933, private lending institutions across the country had failed, and sur-
viving mortgage lenders were severely curtailing their lending. Hundreds of
thousands of borrowers sought refinancing. To families that defaulted on
their mortgage debts, the damage went well beyond the loss of property and
savings invested in their homes. In Senate testimony, a New York mortgage
industry official noted how often foreclosures struck "despair in the heart of
the wife. It brings illnesses on. We contact cases that are virtually mental bor-
derline cases." Sometimes "malnutrition [is] brought on by making oversize

[mortgage] payments at the deprivation of [food on] the table."[2] The emotional distress to a family of losing its home should not be overlooked.

Hundreds of boxes containing the HOLC's correspondence at the National Archives yield many stories like Anna's. The HOLC described its borrowers as "in trouble through no fault of their own," and its internal correspondence backs that claim up. A real estate broker in Detroit, Lee Crane, was "living on money contributed to him by his mother" when he applied to the HOLC for refinancing in 1933. His business failed as the real estate industry fell apart. The bad economy forced his lender, the National Life Insurance Company of the United States of America, to foreclose on his mortgage in April 1933. By Michigan law he had the option to regain ownership if he could pay the amount he owed on the mortgage during the "redemption period," which lasted two years, until April 1935. Since his lender could not sell the property during that period, Lee was able to stay in the house as a rent tenant. He sought ways to borrow the funds necessary to exercise his redemption option, but mortgage credit was scarce; in fact, according to a federal report, none of the Detroit-area lenders were "making any mortgage loans whatsoever at this time." Eventually, Lee was able to find a new job (with the HOLC, in fact), but he still could not find a lender that would lend him the funds to pay off his old debt and buy back his property. One reason was that he still owed three years' worth of back taxes on the property. The HOLC's mortgage refinance program provided him the opportunity to stay in the house and get back on track toward paying off what he owed.[3]

Raymond Carswell had worked in the executive offices of department stores for twenty years. By 1933, though, Raymond had been out of work so long that he was "on his uppers," an old euphemism about someone being in such dire straits that their shoe soles had completely worn out. He was being considered for management at a large department store, but that job was likely to materialize only when the economy improved, and until then he was spending much time and expense attempting to make a contact anywhere in the country. With his deep experience, he was hoping that there would be a "recognition that gray hair carries something that is lacking in black hair stem." Raymond had "his chin up," but without a source of income he came to owe two years of taxes and interest on his mortgage. He thought he might be able to keep the house for a while if his daughter and her husband moved in and contributed to the mortgage payments. Yet this would not pay off the back debt, and with his lender considering foreclosure, Raymond was in grave danger of losing his home. The HOLC eventually stepped in to save Raymond's home.[4]

To deliver relief to these borrowers, the HOLC changed how the debt was paid back and, in some cases, lowered the amount of debt itself.

## Changing How Debts Were Repaid

Fundamentally, the HOLC offered relief by simply acting as a lender at a time when existing lenders were informing their borrowers that their cases had no hope and that the lenders were no longer interested in carrying them.

Affordable monthly payments were important in keeping borrowers away from foreclosure. The form of relief the HOLC offered in this regard depended on the structure of borrowers' previous loans. Among the broad menu of loans offered in the 1920s, we compare the HOLC loan with two common loans. The first is a short-term interest-only loan lasting five years; loan lengths often ranged from two to six years. Since this loan required only interest payments during the five years, the entire principal debt was left to be repaid or refinanced at the end of the loan. The second was a loan offered by B&Ls that featured equal payments each month, usually for a period of about eleven to thirteen years. Technically, these payments would be used to buy shares in the B&L, and when those shares finally totaled the amount of the principal, the principal was repaid and the B&L's lien on the property removed.

Borrowers faced problems with each of these loans in the 1930s. Although borrowers could typically refinance short-term loans with ease in normal times, lenders in the frozen mortgage market of the early 1930s often asked borrowers to pay down a substantial amount of the outstanding principal, or to fully repay the principal when short-term loans reached maturity.[5] With refinancing difficult, many borrowers fell into delinquency. In the case of the B&L loan, as B&L profitability fell, so did the value of B&L shares in which loan repayments were invested. As a result, a borrower in good standing saw the value of shares that he had paid into the sinking fund fall in value. Since he could not pay off the principal of the loan until the value of the shares added up to the principal, he had to make more payments than expected to pay off the principal and obtain full ownership of the home.

For those with the B&L loan, one of the HOLC contract's strongest forms of relief came from an option to reduce monthly payments for the first three years, while times were still tough, by not paying any principal. These three years lasted from June 13, 1933, to June 13, 1936, that is, the first three years after the HOLC Act was passed rather than the first three years of any given borrower's loan. This forbearance option was available at the borrower's discretion until April 1934 and "was claimed by practically all" borrowers who received loans up to that point. In April 1934, Congress opted to put such decisions under the discretion of the HOLC instead.[6] Regardless, throughout the program, the HOLC retained the power to grant extensions on principal or interest at any time according to the judgment of its officials, and members of Congress indicated that they believed the forbearance option was unnecessary given this authority. During the three-year period without principal payments, an HOLC loan was easier for the borrower to handle than, for example, a B&L loan, which would have continued to require share purchases along with the interest payment each month. The forbearance option given by the HOLC was not free, though, because the loan still needed to be paid off in fifteen years. After those first three years, payments rose enough so that borrowers could fully repay the principal over the remaining life of their fifteen-year contracts.

The idea behind the three-year moratorium on principal payments was that the borrower would be in a better position to repay after three years. In fact, the economy did improve some in the mid-1930s, as unemployment rates had fallen from 25 to 14 percent from 1934 to 1937, but unemployment rates of 14 percent meant that many people were still in tough economic times.[7] In addition, this three-year option probably made less of a difference for borrowers who previously had short-term interest-only loans, as they were not paying regular payments to retire principal on those loans. Indeed, if borrowers were not able to pay the monthly payments on interest-only loans, there would be little hope they would be able to make the monthly payments on the HOLC loans either. However, these borrowers were likely in trouble because their lenders were demanding repayment of a substantial portion, or the entire amount, of their original loan.

Other features of the HOLC loan delivered relief, including the loan-to-value ratio, the interest rate, the payment plan, and the length. First mortgage loans during the 1920s were typically limited to 40 – 60 percent of property value, whereas HOLC loans had a higher limit of 80 percent. This eliminated the need for borrowers to find second mortgages at interest rates of 11 or

12 percent in order to borrow larger amounts. The HOLC charged an interest rate of 5 percent, notably below the rates available from private lenders at the time. For example, a national survey of sixty-four cities in 1934 found that most interest rates on existing first mortgages were between 6 and 8 percent. To show how all of these features brought substantial relief to borrowers, table 8.1 compares the HOLC loan with loans from the 1920s and early 1930s.

In terms of the payment plan, the HOLC's loan was in many ways more like a B&L loan than a short-term loan. Like the B&L loan, the HOLC loan featured equal payments each month that would gradually repay the entire debt. The length of the HOLC was a bit longer, so the monthly payments could be a bit smaller. The other major difference was the treatment of the monthly payments. Recall that B&L borrowers paid down the principal on their loans by buying B&L shares on monthly installments, which served as a sinking fund until enough was accumulated to pay the entire principal. The principal was

**Table 8.1. Terms on HOLC loans and common private-sector loans in the 1920s**

| | HOLC loan | Common short-term loan | Typical B&L loan |
|---|---|---|---|
| Interest rate[a] | 5% | 6–8% | 6–8% |
| Length | 15 years | 5 years | 11–12 years |
| Payment plan | Equal payments each month that paid interest and gradually extinguished debt | Interest payments only; entire principal paid or refinanced at end of contract | Equal payments each month that paid interest and gradually accumulated B&L membership shar |
| Maximum loan-to-value ratio | 80% | 60% | 60% |
| Other features | Option for interest-only payments until June 1936, then slightly higher payments | | Length and cost not certain: depended on profitability of the B&L as a whole |

[a]Effective interest rates are from Wickens (1941, 250), which contains Civil Works Administration surveys for cities taken in January 1934.

then repaid at that time. These investments remained at risk, therefore, in contrast to the monthly principal payments on an HOLC loan, which were immediately applied to reducing the amount of principal owed each month. Unlike the B&L borrower, therefore, the HOLC borrower knew for sure that the loan repayment would last only fifteen years.

To demonstrate the difference created by the HOLC loan plan, table 8.2 builds on the example of Joshua Clark's debt from chapter 1 and summarizes the experience he would have had with six different payment plans, including the two private-sector loan plans just mentioned and four variants of the HOLC contract.

Recall that Joshua owed a total debt of $2,272 when he refinanced in 1935, and that he had been paying 8 percent interest on his defaulted loan, which at the time was the prevailing market rate in nearby Boise, Idaho.[8] In interpreting the table, keep in mind that Joshua's income in 1933 was about $100 a month, higher than in the previous two years but below his earnings during the 1920s. Beside his mortgage debt, he also had the burden of medical debt that is not included in the table. The average monthly income for home owners in Boise at the time was around $96, so Joshua is close to a typical case.[9]

The first two lines of table 8.2 compare the two loans with the lowest monthly payments that a distressed borrower like Joshua could have hoped for. A five-year balloon loan (line A) from the private sector with an interest rate of 8 percent would have required a monthly interest payment of $15.15 and repayment of the entire principal of $2,272 in 1940. He could try to refinance again in 1940, but Joshua and all other borrowers who had faced so much trouble refinancing between 1932 and 1935 would have seen this as a risky proposition. Nevertheless, he probably would have taken such a loan if it were offered to him and if the HOLC had not existed. Joshua may not have viewed refinancing in 1940 as all that risky since most Americans would have had little experience to tell them that the economy would remain depressed for the rest of the decade.

The HOLC loan with interest-only payments until June 1936 (line B) required a considerably lower monthly payment of $9.47 during the first eighteen months. The forbearance period lasted only eighteen months because Joshua's loan started in January 1935, relatively late for the HOLC. Whether Joshua actually received this initial forbearance period is unclear from the

**Table 8.2. Monthly payments required by different types of loans with principal of $2,272**

| | Type of loan | Years to repay | Interest rate (%) | Monthly payment, Jan. 1935– June 1936 | Monthly payment, July 1936 to end of loan | Balance in Jan. 1940 |
|---|---|---|---|---|---|---|
| A | Interest-only balloon loan | 5 | 8 | $15.15 | $15.15 | $2,272 |
| B | HOLC loan with interest only payments until June 1936 and amortized payments thereafter | 15 | 5 | $9.47 | $19.31 | $1,821 |
| C | B&L loan with equal monthly payments | 11–13 | 8 | $26.65 | $26.65 | $1,444– 1,582 |
| D | Amortized HOLC loan | 15 | 5 | $17.97 | $17.97 | $1,704 |
| E | Amortized HOLC loan at market rate | 15 | 8 | $21.71 | $21.71 | $2,047 |
| F | Like row D, with liberalized terms after August 1939 | 25 | 4.5 | $17.97 | $10.95 | $1,730 |

records we have; because his loan is dated after April 1934, the decision was up to the HOLC and not necessarily a privilege for every borrower after that date. This initial monthly payment is lower than the payment required by the private-sector interest-only loan because of the lower interest rate on the HOLC loan. The difference is fairly large, showing the extent to which the HOLC's low interest rates really did make a difference for its borrowers. Joshua's required payments would have jumped to $19.31 in July 1937, though, when the HOLC began to require regular amortization payments. If he was unable to meet this condition, he once again would face foreclosure, but the HOLC had the authority to extend his payments at their discretion. If he was successful in meeting the payments, on the other hand, by 1940 his payments would have reduced the loan balance from the original principal of $2,722 to $1,821. He would also have this payment locked in, so that he could continue to pay $19.31 a month until the loan was fully repaid on January 1, 1950. This HOLC loan, therefore, provided borrowers with very low-cost mortgages during this period of extreme distress, and an opportunity for permanent refinancing.

Had Joshua commanded sufficient income and resources in 1935, he might have preferred to pay more of the principal debt immediately. In the private sector, a B&L share-accumulation loan (line C) would have provided him such a payment plan. Under this arrangement, Joshua would have simultaneously taken out an interest-only balloon loan of $2,272 with the monthly interest payment of $15.15 and pledged to purchase $2,272 in B&L shares with payments for the shares spread over equal value of shares in monthly installments (twenty-three shares with $100 maturity value each, for example). We have assumed in the table that Joshua's association, like most others, would have required him to pay $0.50 each month on each of the twenty-three shares, totaling an additional $11.50 each month. Therefore, the total monthly payment would have been about $26.65. The value of Joshua's shares would have grown over time as these installment payments accumulated and dividends were paid on his existing balances. When his share accumulations reached their face value of $100, these would be used to pay off the entire loan. The dividends paid on shares were uncertain, of course, and we calculate the remaining balance on the combined loan and share contracts in this case by assuming semiannual dividend payments in a range from a minimum of 0 percent (leaving $1,582 of principal) to a maximum of 8 percent (leaving $1,444 of principal). In the latter case Joshua's loan would have been paid off after eleven years, while the duration would have been thirteen years if dividends were paid at the lower 0 percent rate.

Line D in the table shows the monthly payments for the HOLC's standard fifteen-year, fully amortized loan without any initial forbearance on principal payments. In this case the HOLC contract provided relief in the form of a monthly payment that would have been one-third lower than the payment on the B&L loan, with the difference attributable to the HOLC loan's longer amortization period and its lower interest rate. To give a sense for the importance of the HOLC's interest rate subsidy by itself, line E gives the monthly payment that would have been required at market interest rates but with the same fifteen-year duration. In either case, the HOLC's loan was much more affordable than the B&L loan on a monthly basis, while still providing amortization. In fact, the HOLC loan was only a few dollars a month more expensive than the interest-only loan in line A. Compared to the B&L loan, another advantage was that the amount outstanding in 1940 would have been known in advance with certainty. The HOLC loan also had a liberal prepayment feature, so its borrowers could pay the loan off as quickly as their resources allowed with no additional cost.

HOLC loan terms were liberalized even more in 1939, as discussed below, after the unemployment rate had spiked to 19 percent during 1938, and after many borrowers demonstrated difficulty in meeting the higher payments that kicked in after June 1936. After August 1939, the HOLC allowed loan durations to be extended up to twenty-five years, and it lowered the interest rate on all of its loans to 4.5 percent. The new loan terms lowered Joshua's monthly payment to $10.95 (line F in table 8.2), while delaying the time to full ownership of the home for an additional ten years. The corporation practiced even more leniency during the war buildup by reducing payments required for families who were in danger of falling behind because of lost income when a family member was inducted into the military.[10]

Altogether, HOLC loans provided borrowers with clear advantages relative to private alternatives, especially for borrowers who were in distress in 1933 and 1934. It is also important to keep in mind that private lenders were not eager to make new loans in many, if not most, local markets in 1934. If they had been willing and able, they would have almost certainly offered much less attractive terms to a borrower like Joshua Clark, who had medical debts, owed back interest and tax payments, and who needed to put new roof shingles and fresh paint on his property.

Given the debt that Joshua had to refinance with the HOLC and the drops in housing values, it seems that Joshua potentially could have been better off by not applying to the HOLC, and instead giving up the house to foreclosure and rebuying it in a distress sale. For example, say the distress sale cut the house price to $1,500. By not applying to the HOLC, maybe Joshua could have bought the house for $1,500 and avoided having to repay the $333 in missed loan payments and the $379 in taxes and insurance. Although this sounds as if he could have avoided his debts, he faced two problems. First, the lender might sue him for a deficiency judgment. Second, where was he going to get the money for the purchase price? If no one was going to lend him money for the refinance, once any lender discovered Joshua's scheme, they were even less likely to lend him money for the repurchase.

HOLC borrowers who had consistently made their loan payments had built up a good credit history, making them attractive to other lenders. By not charging a penalty for early payment, the HOLC encouraged borrowers to pay off their loans early. By 1941 roughly 8 percent of the loans had been fully paid off; by the end of the war in 1945, 30 percent had been prepaid. This benefited the HOLC as well, because reductions in the number of loans they serviced meant they could cut staff.[11]

To help borrowers stay current on their taxes and insurance, the HOLC also provided additional services. In the late 1930s the HOLC made advances to its borrowers for the purpose of paying insurance bills or taxes. This ensured that borrowers did not lose their homes due to tax troubles or lose their savings due to a disaster. Later the HOLC provided an alternative service in which it collected extra monthly amounts to cover taxes and insurance, similar to the way modern loans typically create escrow accounts for those purposes. In 1945 this service was being provided to roughly two-thirds of the HOLC's borrowers. The HOLC found this practice less costly than having to search through tax and insurance records for delinquencies if a borrower fell further behind on loan payments.[12]

## The Debts Home Owners Needed to Refinance

We turn now to the *amount* of debt to be repaid, rather than *how* repayment of the debt was structured. Delinquent mortgage borrowers accumulated a variety of debts beyond their original loans. Missed interest payments added up over time, and property taxes fell by the wayside, especially in this earlier era when loan servicers did not keep constant tabs on tax payments as they do today. Sometimes lenders stepped in to pay these taxes and prevent the property from being seized by a local government, but a borrower would eventually need to compensate their lender for this. Often, borrowers also delayed important maintenance and repair jobs on their houses and properties.

As seen in chapter 7, when the HOLC negotiated with lenders, it tried to offer them attractive prices. This usually involved paying first mortgage holders nearly all the principal and interest they were owed, as well as any back property taxes on the property. The loans also funded critical repairs when necessary. These policies led to HOLC loans that were written for higher amounts than on the borrower's previous mortgage loans, although the borrower's total debt was not increased by the consolidation.

A good way to illustrate how debt loads accumulated is to return to the example of Joshua Clark. He originally borrowed $1,250 from the Citizens Savings and Loan Society in May 1929 at an 8 percent interest rate. By the time the HOLC refinanced his mortgage, all of his debts added up to $2,272. Table 8.3 contains a summary of these debts, all of which require a bit of explanation.

The first line of table 8.3 indicates that Joshua still owed $1,149 of his principal debt, which started at $1,250. In fact, he never made any principal payments, but at some point his lender appears to have insisted that he liquidate an insurance policy to reduce his debt. It should be noted that Joshua's contract had not required principal payments, either. The loan had one of the short-term contracts described above. It was scheduled to last for three years, calling for interest payments of $8.33 each month but no principal payments until the entire principal of $1,250 came due and could be renewed in May 1932. In terms of the interest payments, Joshua had made sixteen monthly payments until stopping in October 1931. From October 1931 until February 1935 when the HOLC refinanced his loan, Joshua missed forty monthly interest payments of $8.33, totaling $341.67.

Five years of unpaid taxes were a nontrivial part of Joshua's debt, adding up to $416 by the time the HOLC closed the loan in February 1935. The house had fallen into disrepair, as Joshua clearly did not have the funds to cover the costs of fixing it up. As a result, the HOLC added another $310 for repairs it considered necessary to protect the value of the home as collateral—a new roof and paint for the outside walls. Finally, $55 in closing costs rounded out the total to $2,272.

It is worth pausing here to note the good deal that HOLC was able to give

**Table 8.3. Sources of Joshua Clark's debt, refinanced by the HOLC in February 1935**

| Source of debt | Amount |
| --- | --- |
| Outstanding loan amount (principal) | $1,149 |
| 40 months of missed interest payments ($8.33 per month from October 1931 to February 1935) | $342 |
| City and county property taxes and insurance costs, 1929–1930 (paid by lender) | $126 |
| City and county property taxes, 1931–1934 (unpaid) | $290 |
| Funds for repairs provided by the HOLC | $310 |
| Closing costs on the HOLC loan | $55 |
| Total | $2,272 |

*Source*: Home Owners' Loan Corporation Papers, Regional Correspondence, Box 150, National Archives II, College Park, MD.

Joshua's lender, Citizens Savings and Loan. Citizens received every last cent of principal debt and accrued interest owed and was fully compensated for the taxes that it had paid to protect its collateral from seizure by the city or county. In turn, Joshua received no debt reduction, because he was the sort of borrower whose debts fell below the 80 percent limit discussed in chapter 7. As a result, the HOLC did not ask his lender to forgive any debt.

Joshua Clark's case also underscores why HOLC loans were not made to remedy recklessness by individual borrowers. When Joshua purchased the house in 1929, he had paid $3,000. The house likely fell in value over the next four years. In nearby Boise, Idaho, for example, the average value of single-family homes fell by 25.5 percent. A similar fall in Coeur d'Alene prices would have cut the value of Joshua's house to $2,235, slightly less than the principal of $2,272 on the new HOLC loan.[13] In 1929, Joshua had paid for more than half of his house in cash, but lost a substantial chunk of that equity after not having paid taxes or interest for such a long time. Joshua, like most HOLC borrowers, was largely a victim of reduced income and housing prices from the Depression, and of the large debts imposed on him by his wife's illness.

The HOLC judged the market value of Joshua's house as $2,500 but raised it to $2,850, given the new repairs that were made. With a loan of $2,272 from the HOLC (including the $310 in repairs), Joshua's debt load relative to market value in 1935 was roughly 79 percent, right around the norm for HOLC borrowers. In general, the best evidence available on borrowers' debt burdens comes from a sample of HOLC loans from Connecticut, New Jersey, and New York that was provided to C. Lowell Harriss and the National Bureau of Economic Research in the early 1950s. Figure 8.1 shows the distribution of the debt loads as a percentage of the mid-1930s market price estimated by HOLC officials at the time of each borrower's application. These price estimates are estimates of current market value, which is not necessarily the same as the HOLC appraisals, which were designed to estimate longer-run value.[14] The debt load came from unpaid interest, taxes, insurance, costs of repair, and the principal necessary to finish the loan, as for Joshua. While Joshua had

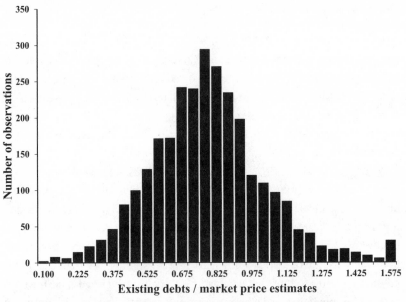

**Figure 8.1.** *Distribution of existing debt burdens relative to market prices for HOLC borrowers. The market prices were estimated by the HOLC. Existing debts include principal debts and unpaid interest and taxes. (Sample of HOLC loans in New York, New Jersey, and Connecticut. Data from National Bureau of Economic Research 1947.)*

only one mortgage loan, about 40 percent of the borrowers in the sample had a second mortgage loan as well.

One reason that the average HOLC borrower had a debt load around 80 percent of mid-1930s property value was that first mortgage loans allowed these people to borrow up to only 50 or 60 percent of the value of their homes. With housing prices having fallen a long way, and with enough mortgage and tax payments missed, it is easy to conceive of a 20–30 percentage-point increase in debts relative to the value of the property. If borrowers had second mortgages and incurred some additional tax debts or other debts, they could easily fall into the higher indebtedness range in the right side of figure 8.1. More of these borrowers likely existed but were not served by the HOLC, as debt forgiveness would have been required by their lenders. Unfortunately, we have never been able to find data on rejected applications aside from what is shown in table 7.1 (see p. 73), which suggests that perhaps 18 percent of borrowers were rejected because their debts were too high and their lenders refused to forgive enough of it.

Roughly 20 percent of the HOLC borrowers in the tristate sample mentioned above were underwater when they approached the HOLC. They were in especially fragile positions if they were unable to make their regular mortgage payments, because they could not fully pay off their debt simply by selling their properties. This essentially barred them from refinancing through the private sector, making them natural candidates for refinancing through the HOLC. In these cases, the HOLC would have been forced to negotiate with lenders for some debt forgiveness.

In Joshua's case, the HOLC estimated his property's market value at $2,500, while the appraisal ended up only a bit higher at $2,540. Of course, this is consistent with what we know about HOLC appraisals—they were more likely to raise the final appraisal significantly above market price if the appraisal was going to be a deciding factor in what they could pay lenders. In Joshua's case, they were able to pay his lender 100 percent of what was owed, so there was no need to adjust the appraisal upward too much in order to enlist the lender's participation. Nevertheless, the appraisal policies put in place did result in an appraisal slightly higher than the estimated market price.

Even though Joshua's loan amount came in under the 80 percent loan-to-appraisal ratio, there were still quite a few borrowers whose accumulated debts were more than 80 percent of the appraisals. In these cases, lenders granted debt reductions to avoid going over the 80 percent figure. The key constraint on the HOLC's ability to accept such cases was the need to induce lender participation. Principal reductions occurred only if lenders forgave the debt, as the HOLC was not willing take immediate losses of this sort. In about 50 percent of the mortgages in the tristate sample, the borrowers had their debt loads reduced by varying amounts to bring the principal on the new HOLC loan into line with the 80 percent ratio to the appraisal of long-run value. The amounts typically forgiven were not large, but the sheer number of cases in which debt was partially forgiven suggests a sizable subsidy to borrowers. The HOLC estimated that across all of its loans, 7 percent of borrowers' outstanding debts were forgiven, on average.[15]

To modern readers, figure 8.1 may be surprising, even confusing, as it shows that slightly more than half of the HOLC's borrowers had substantial equity in their properties, that is, owed debts that added up to less than 80 percent of their property's estimated market values. It seems that they ought to have been able to sell their homes for enough money to clear their debts and therefore avoid foreclosure. One factor to keep in mind, though, is the defunct state of credit markets in this period. Mortgage borrowers could only have sold their homes if buyers could have obtained loans to finance their purchases. The market prices in figure 8.1 are estimates using prices from market transactions of similar properties. By definition, those are transactions in which buyers actually did obtain loans, but such was the inexact science of appraisals in a deeply dysfunctional housing market that no borrower could have been sure of finding a buyer able to pay the same price because no buyer could have been assured of obtaining a loan. In contrast, in the years since 2008, the modern mortgage loan market has had a significant backstop in the presence of Fannie Mae and Freddie Mac, which (due to the backing of the US Treasury) have been able to buy loans from all types of lenders that meet the two companies' underwriting standards. This has helped keep the loan market alive, but no similar backstops existed during the early 1930s. These factors may explain why so many borrowers with relatively low debts still ended up refinancing with the HOLC, as it was the only creditor in town.

### The HOLC's Leniency in Dealing with Widespread Delinquencies

With unemployment rates remaining high through the end of the 1930s, times were still tough for many HOLC borrowers. By July 1936, three years

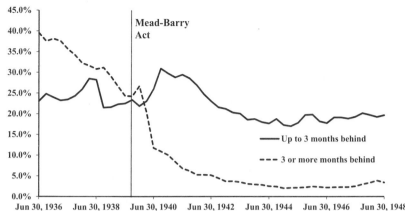

**Figure 8.2.** *Percent of outstanding HOLC borrowers behind on payments. Data before June 1936 are not available (Harriss 1951, 201).*

into the HOLC program, nearly 40 percent of borrowers were more than three months behind in their payments on their HOLC loans, and this rate was still 35 percent the next year (figure 8.2). The HOLC eventually foreclosed on only about 19.4 percent of its borrowers, however.

Delinquencies were high in 1936 partly because the temporary three-year forbearance period ended. When the forbearance period ended in June 1936, unemployment was lower than in 1933 but still widespread, and many borrowers could not afford the higher monthly payments. Most HOLC foreclosures took place in the few years after 1936.[16] This was a major problem for the HOLC, and sentiment in Congress built up for a moratorium on HOLC foreclosures, though none was ever implemented.[17] Without action, it looked like the HOLC experiment could have ended in widespread foreclosure, just what it was trying to avoid.

Ultimately, the foreclosure rate totaled 19 percent, a significant rate but much lower than the delinquency rate of over 65 percent in early 1936. Without a doubt, a great help came from the economic growth after the 1937–1938 recession that continued into the 1940s, and more help came from the increase in house prices during the war years. Some of the improvement is also likely attributable to a further liberalization of loan terms in 1939 as a result of new legislation. In that year, the Mead-Barry Act allowed the HOLC to extend its loans' durations to as long as twenty-five years. The HOLC, by a vote of its board, also lowered its loan interest rates to 4.5 percent from 5 percent.[18] About one-quarter of the HOLC's original loans had their durations extended, many after extended periods of delinquency.[19] In fact, about half of the extended loans had been in arrears by twelve months or more. After extension, the HOLC treated all extended loans as new loans, thereby erasing past delinquencies and providing borrowers with yet another chance to start over.

These liberalizations explain the rapid drop in serious delinquencies in figure 8.2 (the dashed line) in the months after the Mead-Barry bill was made into law. They also explain the increase in short-run delinquencies (the solid line), as some of the borrowers fell behind on their loan payments once again. Nevertheless, serious delinquencies were never again as large a problem for the HOLC, as the dashed line fell to low levels and stayed there. Borrowers found their monthly payments to be more affordable because of the longer amortization period and lower interest rates. Economic recovery, before and after the buildup to the war, likely helped buoy borrowers' incomes as well. Housing prices also rose during the war, due to restrictions on new construction.

On those loans it foreclosed, HOLC officials clearly gave borrowers a long time in which to avoid foreclosure. Instead of moving these borrowers quickly into foreclosure, the HOLC practiced a great deal of patience, delaying foreclosure as long as a loan had any hope. The HOLC was known as a lenient servicer, although some contemporaries disagreed with that statement, and certainly not every borrower's experience was the same. In particular, the HOLC was slow to foreclose when borrowers fell behind on their loan payments. Many of the HOLC loan officers acted as social workers in helping borrowers find jobs or obtain work relief and other resources through other government programs.[20] In 88 percent of the nearly 100,000 foreclosures that had occurred by July 1937, HOLC loan service officers held off taking the action for more than a year after borrowers had stopped making mortgage and tax payments. They waited more than eighteen months in 63 percent of the cases.[21] Some foreclosures were inevitable, regardless, as nearly a quarter of foreclosures occurred in cases where the houses had been abandoned or the owners died and their heirs refused to assume the mortgages.

This leniency before foreclosure continued in the late 1930s and the 1940s, but the speed of foreclosure picked up a bit compared to earlier practice. Of the foreclosures that had occurred by 1941 (almost all of the HOLC's eventual total), the loan officers waited more than a year after delinquency to foreclose in 64 percent of the cases (as compared to 88 percent of the cases up to July 1937), and more than two years in 24 percent.[22]

As an example of the HOLC's servicing practices, documents in the HOLC collection at the National Archives describe the story of Frank White from Los Angeles, an HOLC borrower who suffered an eye injury that laid him up for a year and caused him to fall behind by about $150 on payments for taxes and street assessments. Using its authority to extend payments "if the circumstances of the home owner justify such an extension," the HOLC accepted lower payments during that year. The HOLC loan officer supported him because his attitude was "excellent and pride of home ownership is borne out by condition of home and grounds." He was demonstrating good faith by "raising rabbits, chickens, and pigeons to help with living," and once he returned to work, the loan officer expressed confidence that Frank's "account will rapidly be brought up to date and the slate cleared of all delinquencies." This was part of a pattern of behavior in which the HOLC looked beyond a borrower's payment history and focused more on the character of the borrower and ability to pay in the future.[23]

This leniency had its limits, though. When borrowers failed to demonstrate good character, the HOLC was just as punishing as a private lender would have been. After borrowing from the HOLC, Katherin Cooper of Whitman, Massachusetts, was confined to the Taunton Hospital for the Insane, and her mortgage payments to the HOLC soon stopped. The field representative suspected that the father owned the home and was using his daughter's mental illness to avoid repaying the loan, describing Katherin as "a straw for her father. This is substantiated by the fact the father is collecting rent, but he will not admit ownership." Eventually, with knowledge of the father's behavior, HOLC officials decided to foreclose. This case also exemplifies the difficulty that lenders had in collecting information about their borrowers, even when the lender had the time, patience, and resources that the HOLC did. Some decisions were inevitably difficult because HOLC loan officers had trouble determining the exact circumstances underlying default.[24]

Those at the receiving end of skeptical treatment from the HOLC likely did not appreciate it. One critic of the HOLC described it as a lender that "viewed almost every default as a prima-facie effort to cheat the government."[25] This, it seems, is a bit of an exaggeration, yet it likely reflects the attitude of some loan officers with certain borrowers. It also captures the tricky politics inherent to a government-backed entity foreclosing loans on its own citizens.

Once the HOLC had foreclosed, the officials had to decide whether to pursue a deficiency judgment, which involves suing the borrower for the difference between her debt and the proceeds received from the sale of the property via foreclosure. In practice, these decisions appear to have been conducted on the basis that any lender would conduct them, whether or not the deficiency judgments were likely to yield any income. For example, the HOLC did not seek a deficiency judgment against Antonio Cristiano from West New York, New Jersey, because they decided it would have been fruitless. The HOLC official reviewing the case argued that Cristiano was "too old to work, and the possibility of the 17 year old nephew procuring work, which would not be sufficient to liquidate, cannot be expected. Efforts have been made to sell, and the property has been listed, with no results." Cristiano could "not make any payment plan. He seems to have a number of relatives to support, and they pay nothing towards maintenance of household." Cristiano had tried to rent some rooms to generate income, but claimed that his tenants had been delinquent in paying the rent for three months. Ultimately, he conveyed the home to the HOLC, and no deficiency judgment was sought.[26]

Similarly, Miriam Connor had obtained an HOLC loan on a house in Ocean City, New Jersey, but she had been required to move to Philadelphia to find a job even before the loan was closed. In the field representative's view, "All efforts to rehabilitate [the] loan have failed. The home owner appears to be hopelessly in debt, her arrears totaling over $1200. . . . She states that she cannot meet the expenses on the property and does not intend to live there again, and is willing to give a deed to the HOLC." Since the market value of the property was less than the debt owed, the HOLC accepted the deed to the home and did not pursue a deficiency judgment.[27]

On the other hand, HOLC loan officers were quite unsympathetic with borrowers who had sufficient assets or income to pay the HOLC but remained delinquent, and pursued deficiency judgments in those cases. When refinancing in November 1934, Edwin Corday, of Memphis, Tennessee, elected for the fifteen-year loan with a monthly payment of $78 for a home that was worth roughly four times the value of the home of Joshua Clark, discussed earlier. Even after switching to the option to pay only interest until 1936, Edwin was delinquent on his payments and had not paid his taxes for two years. When the borrower offered to give up the house to cover his debt to the HOLC, the district service supervisor investigated and discovered that the borrower was "planning to purchase the property next door as quickly as he is released from his obligation to the Corporation," and thus was no more than a "typical chiseler." HOLC officials decided to foreclose and seek a deficiency judgment for the difference.[28]

## Transition to the Modern Mortgage Contract

From today's perspective, the features of an HOLC mortgage outlined in table 8.1 look fairly standard. Many mortgage borrowers today can almost take for granted the availability of a conventional fifteen-year loan, at 5 percent interest, for 80 percent of the value of the property, and with regular monthly payments on both principal and interest. In fact, this would be a relatively conservative loan by today's standards. When the HOLC adopted this loan for its borrowers, though, it was unusual. The closest approximation was probably the traditional loan from a B&L, but these loans did not truly pay off the principal each month, instead allowing borrowers to buy equity shares in the B&L. The whole structure had been popular and successful for decades but utterly fell apart during the Depression. Other loan contracts, typically with terms up to five years and featuring no regular payments except for interest, likewise had their deficiencies exposed.

The fundamental change in the contract terms that the HOLC offered borrowers is critical to understanding how it gave both lenders and borrowers good deals. The federal guarantees, funded by taxpayers, permitted the agency to write loans with much more liberal lending terms than existing loans, including lower interest rates. As a result, the HOLC was able to give lenders a good deal while borrowers benefited with loans that offered lower monthly payments, longer terms to maturity, and lower risk than the loans they had originally signed.

The HOLC's role in the evolution of the modern residential mortgage contracts is a subject of interest in its own right. These modern loan contracts have a history dating back to the 1880s in the US residential mortgage market, and earlier in foreign residential markets and in farm markets.[29] The HOLC's adoption was part of a broad change in contracts across the mortgage finance industry during the 1930s, driven by dissatisfaction with the existing contracts in light of the burdens they placed on borrowers after 1929. However, we do not want to overstate the HOLC's contribution here. The HOLC did not compete with private lenders, and therefore it is difficult to explain changes in contract use among private lenders on the basis of the HOLC's competitive influence. The modern loan contract was adopted widely by the private sector over the rest of the 1930s for a variety of reasons, and by the 1940s such loans dominated the industry. In general, the primary impact of the HOLC's adoption of this loan contract came through demonstrations that the contract could be used successfully in a large number of cases. After all, the HOLC provided this type of loan to 20 percent of all mortgaged nonfarm home owners in America in the mid-1930s.

# CHAPTER 9

# REPAIRING
# MORTGAGE
# AND HOUSING
# MARKETS

The goals of the HOLC reached beyond the provision of relief to individual lenders and borrowers. HOLC officials were also determined to systematically stabilize mortgage and housing markets by interrupting the vicious cycle of foreclosures and price declines that gripped the country in the early 1930s. By the time the HOLC had begun making loans in late 1933, "foreclosures numbered nearly a thousand a day, the highest in the country's history."[1] Between 1930 and 1934, housing values dropped like a stone. Different regions experienced different price drops, but a survey across forty-eight cities found that the damage was so widespread that the average drop in value was about 32 percent between 1930 and 1934.[2] These price declines propagated additional foreclosures as borrowers lost their jobs and were unable to sell their homes to resolve their debts.

These dynamics were often local. A foreclosure in Michigan was not likely to cause price declines in Massachusetts. Often, business commentators and academics refer to "the" housing market, but we all know that a house in California cannot easily be sold and moved to New York; housing markets necessarily have strong regional attributes. For example, in the early 1930s, homes in Syracuse, Birmingham, San Diego, Lansing, Dallas, and Little Rock had lost an average of more than 40 percent of their resale value. Home owners fared better in Portland (Maine), Providence, Austin, and Topeka, but their houses still lost 20 percent of their value.[3]

Mortgage moratoria were present in some states but not all. They prevented a large number of foreclosures, but were only a stopgap measure to slow the bleeding before something like the HOLC came along. Within this environment the HOLC refinanced loans on one-tenth of the nation's owner-occupied homes and became in three short years its largest residential mortgage lender. Two questions become central to assessing the performance of a program of this size and complexity. First, was the relief provided by the HOLC directed to areas of greatest need? Second, was the relief effective in promoting the program's goals? We examine these two questions in this chapter by broadening our examination of the HOLC's impacts beyond the borrowers and lenders directly affected, to the local housing markets in which they resided and operated.

## The Distribution of HOLC Refinancing

By name and public statements of support, the HOLC was a program designed to assist distressed home owners. The program also was designed to meet the expressed needs of badly damaged home mortgage lenders and to rectify general distress in local housing markets. In the actual implementation of a public program of this scale and complexity, other factors could also have affected how HOLC benefits were distributed throughout the nation. HOLC activity could have been used, for example, to provide general relief to local markets that were being ravaged more by unemployment than by housing distress. Alternatively, HOLC refinancing could have been doled out to curry political favor with voters to the benefit of either national or local politicians. It is also possible, moreover, that the HOLC program was simply badly managed, with relief allocated with little regard for need or eligibility. In any of these cases, the HOLC would likely have had a much weaker effect on foreclosures and the housing crises than if the program had pursued its intended goals.

Across the nation's 3,067 counties, an average of about 14 percent of nonfarm home owners applied for HOLC refinancing, and 48 percent of those were ultimately approved for a loan. There was substantial variation, however, in application and participation rates. Both were higher, for example, in Kootenai County, Idaho, where Joshua Clark was among the 21 percent of home owners (484 in all) who applied for HOLC assistance as well as the 72 percent of applicants (or 377) who were accepted into the program. The HOLC program was even more important in other markets, especially the twenty-five counties in which loans refinanced by the HOLC represented more than one-quarter of the number of nonfarm home owners in 1930. These most active HOLC markets included areas as large and dense as Wayne County, Michigan (Detroit), with a population of nearly two million, and as small as Finney, Kansas (1930 population of 11,104), where the number of HOLC loans equaled just less than one-third of the 845 nonfarm home owners who resided there in 1930.

At the other extreme, no home owners applied for HOLC loans in twenty counties, and no HOLC loans were made in sixty-three. Two-thirds of the counties with no HOLC loans were located in Texas, California, Colorado, Kentucky, or Tennessee. There were also 1,264 counties in which HOLC-refinanced loans represented less than 5 percent of the number of nonfarm owner-occupied homes in 1930. Two of these counties, San Francisco and Hamilton, Ohio, claimed more than 500,000 residents in 1930, and another ninety had 1930 populations greater than 50,000. The remainder of markets in which the HOLC had a relatively low profile had smaller populations and were spread throughout all regions of the country.

A team of scholars used regression analysis to assess the influences that accounted for this marked variation in HOLC application and acceptance rates.[4] Their approach was to determine how differences in measures of general economic distress, housing market conditions, and political influence were related to differences in the intensity of HOLC activity. To isolate the impact of these most important factors, the model also controlled for other characteristics of local markets including the age, race, and marital status of the population; the importance of manufacturing and agriculture to the local economy; and the average level of household income.

In interpreting the results of the analysis, the researchers noted that three parties were involved in each HOLC transaction—the borrower who applied for HOLC refinancing, the original lender who had to agree to sell the loan, and the HOLC staff who determined the eligibility of the borrower and negotiated the purchase price of the original loan. Because these interactions were complex, it is not possible to connect the behavior of any one group to the spatial pattern of HOLC application or acceptance rates. Instead, the regression analysis was designed to uncover how the market conditions in each county affected the interactions among borrowers, lenders, and HOLC staff that determined the rate of HOLC application activity and acceptances.

A central issue in all discussions of New Deal fund distribution has been whether variations in HOLC activity across markets reflected the program's eligibility requirements and responded to the housing distress that it was designed to relieve. The evidence indicates that HOLC performed as intended in both dimensions. Both application and acceptance rates were higher in markets with higher median 1930 home values, a characteristic that should have been associated with both a greater reliance on mortgage financing and stronger post-crisis housing collateral. A strong positive effect of rapid post-1925 building activity also indicated that HOLC applications were higher in markets in which a greater share of homes were under mortgage and remained good prospects for refinancing. Finally, a large positive impact of the 1930 home-ownership rate on the HOLC acceptance rates indicates that HOLC lending was concentrated in more settled, established residential areas where the prospects for successful loan modifications were better than in mixed, transitional neighborhoods.

The analysis also indicates that the relief of housing-specific distress was an important factor in HOLC application and acceptance rates. Areas with more housing distress during the Depression tended to receive more funds, as did areas with more unemployment. Counties with younger populations and higher rates of marriage were also more likely to apply for HOLC refinancing and more likely to obtain it. But most important were measures of housing market distress and housing market characteristics. HOLC funding was positively associated with both higher home prices and higher rates of home ownership. Many studies of total New Deal spending and spending on relief, public works, and farm activity found strong political motivations in the distribution of funds. More was spent in areas where a larger share of the population voted, and where there was more swing voting and more long-run support for Democratic presidential candidates. The HOLC was an unusual program in that many of the patterns of presidential politicking seen in the distribution of funds from other programs did not show up in the study of the allocation of HOLC funds.

A final influence on rates of HOLC activity was the distance between each county and the nearest HOLC office in which the home owner had to apply. Each loan purchase and refinance required multiple meetings with the lender and the borrower, appraisals, visits to the home, and meetings between appraisers and HOLC officials. All of these activities were less costly if the home was in the same community as the HOLC office. They became increasingly costly as people had to travel longer distances. As a result, the regression analysis showed that borrowers were more likely to apply for funds and were more likely to receive funds if they were in or close to counties with HOLC offices. The influence of distance between borrowers and HOLC offices proves to be of great importance in assessing the overall effectiveness of HOLC refinancing.

## The Impact of the HOLC on Local Markets

The HOLC meant to stabilize housing markets by purchasing loans on the verge of foreclosure from lenders and refinancing the loans for the home owners. The goal was to prevent a drop in the demand for owned homes and prevent a fall in the supply of owned homes and a sudden rise in the number of rental properties. Achieving this goal would have led to a positive relationship between the HOLC loans and the number of home owners and the value of homes. This was a heroic undertaking, and so the major question remains and must be asked: Did it work?

Although the HOLC was focused on home ownership and home prices, its activities could have affected other housing market outcomes. Local housing markets, for example, were closely connected to local rental markets, and problems in one could spill into the other. Foreclosed families had to move somewhere, after all, and would have raised the demand for rental housing. The supply of rental housing, on the other hand, could have been augmented if lenders had difficulty selling foreclosed properties and decided instead to rent them out. As the HOLC bought loans from lenders, in addition, it could have effectively increased the supply of new mortgage funds, lowered its cost, and stimulated new construction. In assessing the impacts of the HOLC, therefore, it is important to focus not only on its stated goals of home ownership and housing prices, but also on changes within local rental markets and new residential construction.[5]

In the past few years, two research teams independently examined these issues by compiling and analyzing data on HOLC loan activity, housing markets, and a variety of socioeconomic factors for all of the counties in the United States.[6] The goal in each analysis was to isolate to what extent the introduction of HOLC loans in each county raised housing values and home ownership. To do so each team had to overcome an important obstacle to estimating the true impact of the HOLC impact. We have shown above that HOLC lending was greater in counties that experienced severe housing distress; as a result, we know that HOLC lending volume was positively associated with poorer housing market outcomes. This leads to a problem that arises quite often in program evaluations: it can be difficult to detect a positive impact of greater HOLC activity, given that these funds were disproportionately allocated to local housing markets that were already hardest hit by the crisis. To guard against this possibility, it is necessary to estimate the impact on home ownership and housing prices of variations in HOLC lending volume that were not related to program need. A complete explanation of this problem and its solution is provided in the appendix. The bottom line, however, is that the negative effect of distance between borrowers and HOLC offices provides just the right kind of variation to overcome the problem, because a borrower who lived farther from an office would have been less likely to apply to the HOLC, or to be accepted, for any given level of distress.

Both research teams used the "distance from office" effect to estimate the true impact of the program on home ownership and housing prices and concluded that the HOLC was successful at maintaining the number of home owners and housing values at levels well above where they likely would have ended up without the program.[7] The estimates suggest that a $1 increase in HOLC loans per capita in counties with less than fifty thousand people would have raised housing values by $115.70 in 1940. That same dollar, moreover, would have raised the number of nonfarm home owners by 81.5 people.[8]

The information in table 9.1 shows that, had the HOLC program not existed, the median house value likely would have fallen by $1,078 from $2,278 in 1930 to $1,200 in 1940. Average HOLC lending in the small counties came to about $1.90 per capita. That additional $1.90 would have raised the typical 1940 home value by $231, from $1,200 to $1,431. Therefore, the HOLC helped reduce a potential decline in housing values of 47 percent from $2,278 to $1,200 over the decade of the 1930s to a decline of only 37.2 percent from $2,278 to $1,431. Essentially, it helped eliminate 21.4 percent of the potential decline.

Comparing 1930 to 1940 may actually understate the effectiveness of the HOLC at staving off the decline in housing values. Much of the decline in housing values occurred between 1930 and January 1934, which was about the time the HOLC had begun making loans. The Civil Works Administration survey implied an average drop of about 32 percent in home values during

**Table 9.1. Evaluating the impact of HOLC spending per capita on nonfarm home values and the number of home owners in counties with fewer than fifty thousand people**

Estimated impact of the HOLC on house prices in a typical county, 1930–1940

| | | |
|---|---|---:|
| A | Median house value in 1930 | $2,278 |
| B | Estimated median value in 1940 without the HOLC | $1,200 |
| C | Estimated median house value in 1940 with the HOLC | $1,431 |
| D | Change between 1930 and 1940 without the HOLC (line A − line B) | −$1,078 |
| E | Difference in 1940 value associated with the HOLC (line C − line B) | $231 |
| F | Percentage of potential 1930–1940 decline prevented by the HOLC (line E ÷ line D) | 21% |

Estimated impact of the HOLC on house prices in a typical county, 1934–1940

| | | |
|---|---|---:|
| G | Median house value in 1934 | $1,549 |
| H | Estimated median value without the HOLC in 1940 | $1,200 |
| I | Estimated median value with the HOLC in 1940 | $1,431 |
| J | Change between 1934 and 1940 without the HOLC (line H − line G) | −$349 |
| K | Difference in 1940 value associated with the HOLC (line I − line H) | $231 |
| L | Percentage of potential 1934–1940 decline prevented by the HOLC (line K ÷ line J) | 66% |

Estimated impact of the HOLC on home ownership in a typical county, 1930–1940

| | | |
|---|---|---:|
| M | Number of home owners in 1930 | 1,200 |
| N | Estimated number of home owners in 1940 without the HOLC | 1,223 |
| O | Estimated additional home owners in 1940 due to average HOLC loans per capita | 155 |
| P | Number of home owners in 1940 with the HOLC (line N + line O) | 1,378 |
| Q | Change in number of home owners from 1930 to 1940 with the HOLC (line P − line M) | 178 |
| R | Percentage of 1930–1940 increase in home owners due to the HOLC (line O ÷ line Q) | 87% |

Estimated impact of the HOLC on home ownership in a typical county, 1934–1940

| | | |
|---|---|---:|
| S | Estimated number of home owners in 1934 | 1,164 |
| T | Estimated number of home owners in 1940 without the HOLC | 1,223 |
| U | Estimated additional home owners in 1940 due to average HOLC loans per capita | 155 |
| V | Number of home owners in 1940 with the HOLC (line T + line U) | 1,378 |
| W | Change in number of home owners from 1934 to 1940 with the HOLC (line V − line S) | 214 |
| X | Percentage of 1934–1940 increase in home owners due to the HOLC (line U ÷ line W) | 72% |

that time. If this was the average drop for all counties below fifty thousand people, the typical median value of housing would have fallen from $2,278 in 1930 to $1,549 by the beginning of 1934. Without the HOLC, the typical median house value would have fallen from $1,549 in 1934 to $1,200 in 1940, roughly a loss of $349 in value. An injection of the $1.90 average HOLC spending loans per capita would have raised the 1940 price by $231.40 from $1,200 to $1,431. Thus, the HOLC loans per capita were able to stave off $231 or 69 percent of a potential decline of $349 in housing values between 1934 and 1940.

HOLC activity also helped account for nearly all of the increase in the number of nonfarm home owners in a typical small county over the course of a decade. Without the HOLC average spending of $1.90 per capita, the typical small county would likely have seen a rise in the number of home owners from 1,200 in 1930 to only 1,223 in 1940, an increase of only 23 home owners over the course of the decade. Given that the HOLC had been put in place, the actual rise in the number of home owners was 178, from 1,200 in 1930 to 1,378 in 1940. Table 9.1 shows that the HOLC added an additional 155 home owners in the typical small county and accounted for as much as 87 percent of the rise in the number of home owners between 1930 and 1934.

We do not have comprehensive figures on the number of home owners in US counties during the mid-1930s. Comparisons of 1930 census home-ownership rates to home-ownership rates in a 1934 survey of sixty-one cities by the Civil Works Administration, however, suggest an average drop in the home-ownership rate of about 3 percent. This seems roughly consistent with the rise in foreclosure rates to around 1 percent each year in the early 1930s. Thus, the number of home owners probably fell by about 3 percent between 1930 and the beginning of 1934. If the number of home owners fell 3 percent from the 1930 census average of 1,200, the typical number of home owners would have fallen from 1,200 to 1,164 by 1934. Thus, the typical number of home owners would have risen by 214, from 1,164 in 1934 to 1,378 in 1940. With $1.90 in HOLC spending per capita, the HOLC would have raised the number of home owners by 155, which is about 72 percent of the rise of 214 between 1934 and 1940 in a typical small county.

As successful as the HOLC was in smaller counties, neither research team could find a strong positive effect of the HOLC in counties with more than fifty thousand people in which most HOLC offices were located. There are two potential reasons for this. One possibility is that the "distance from office" strategy, described above and explained more completely in the appendix, was much less effective in larger cities than in smaller cities. We are still working on this issue but have made little headway on it.

The second possibility is that the HOLC might have had little impact in larger cities because there tended to be a stronger network of institutions in the cities that were more effective at backstopping troubled lenders. Thus, the HOLC was needed less in the larger cities than in smaller towns. This situation is similar to what occurred with commercial banks in the 1920s and early 1930s, even though they were not heavily involved in residential mortgage lending. The lion's share of the failures in commercial banks in the 1920s and early 1930s occurred in smaller towns and cities, where there were often only a handful of banks, who all experienced sharp drops simultaneously when the local economy was falling apart.

The statistical analysis of the experience with the HOLC in small counties suggests that the HOLC was a powerful force in staving off declines in home values and home ownership. However, the evidence currently suggests that HOLC activity did not increase building activity. Courtemanche and Snowden examined the issue using information on the year built for every structure reported in the census of 1940. They could find no relationship between the number of homes built after 1934 and HOLC loans per capita. In unpublished work, moreover, neither team could find a positive effect of HOLC lending on the number of building permits before and after the HOLC program in the largest 270 cities in the country.

More work needs to be done in this area, but it does not appear that the replacement of toxic assets on the lenders' books did much to stimulate building construction. One reason may have been that the lenders were still holding a large inventory of foreclosed housing from the early 1930s. This problem was made worse when the HOLC ended up foreclosing on 20 percent of its loans. Thus, builders and lenders may not have seen much opportunity for fruitful investment in home construction during the late 1930s.[9]

# CHAPTER 10

# THE COST TO TAXPAYERS AND SUBSIDIES TO THE HOUSING MARKET

Private investors were not rushing to create their own version of the HOLC in 1933. Anyone with the ability to raise money on the bond market as the HOLC did would have had grave doubts about using that ability to buy up residential mortgages. After all, mortgage lending was a troubled business: lenders saw their balance sheets falling apart after four years of depression, and there seemed to be no end in sight.

This should give us pause when thinking about how the HOLC was financed. The HOLC had a major advantage because it benefited from the backing of the federal government. That was why it was able to tap the bond market so easily. In discussions of the HOLC during recent years, the common conception has been that the HOLC was profitable, and these concerns about taxpayer exposure to the HOLC are typically put aside as unrealized risks. However, our close review in this chapter suggests that if the loan-refinancing program is separated from the HOLC's other activities and if all of its costs are accounted for, it actually was responsible for a small loss to taxpayers. Data from the Comptroller General of the United States, which estimated the HOLC loan program's revenues and costs, indicate that the loan program lost about $53 million, or about 1.8 percent of the roughly $3 billion loaned out through the program. Of course, any evaluation of the program should not be based on these figures alone, as the HOLC had offsetting benefits for lenders, borrowers, and housing markets, as documented in other chapters, as well as additional costs.

The loss would have been larger had the HOLC not been able to borrow as cheaply as it did, with the benefit of the federal guarantee. This reduction in borrowing costs was effectively a net subsidy to housing markets. To gauge the size of the subsidy, had the HOLC been forced to pay an additional 1 percent in interest on its bonds in absence of the federal guarantee, its interest costs would have risen by roughly $300 million, and the subsidy to housing markets would have risen from roughly 2 percent to 12 percent of the value of the loans it made.

## How Much Did the HOLC Cost Taxpayers?

A number of advocates for a new HOLC in the current era have stated that the HOLC loan program made money. To some extent, this discussion is a distraction, as profitability should not be the only consideration, given the wide range of costs and benefits of the program. A loss could be justified if the program delivered large benefits. But it is important to get the facts right.

The claim of profitability appears to have first received national attention in April 1946 and was anticipatory. For example, an article in *Time* on April 22, 1946, stated that "when the Home Owners Loan Corp. was created, Congressional sibyls prophesied that the Government would lose at least $1 billion. Last week HOLC's spry old board chairman, John Henry Fahey, produced figures to show how wrong they had been. When HOLC is finally liquidated in 1948, he said it will show a net profit of some $11,000,000."[1] Since then, the claim has been repeated. David Mason, in his history of the savings and loan industry, cites an article titled "HOLC Closing Out with Profit to U.S." in the *Boston Globe* from April 7, 1946. The claim was also added to the *Wikipedia* entry on the HOLC in July 2007, with citations to a 1979 piece on the HOLC. It then became a key part of the popular conception of the HOLC during public discussions in 2008.[2]

The profitability story seems to gain credence with a quick skim of the HOLC's final report, which states that the US Treasury had established the corporation with a starting capital of $200 million in 1933 and 1934 and that the HOLC repaid $214 million to the Treasury in its final liquidation eighteen years later.[3] At the time, $200 million was a significant sum; it is the equivalent of $3.3 billion in 2010 dollars after adjustment for inflation. However, since the economy has grown much larger over the past several decades, the more relevant comparison is to the size of the economy, as measured by GDP.

A $200 million investment in 1934 was about 0.3 percent of GDP; the same percentage of 2010 GDP would be about $46 billion. The risk to taxpayers was that this $200 million would not be paid back in full if the HOLC lost money. There was a further risk that if the HOLC lost enough money, not only would the federal government lose the $200 million investment, but it might also have had to pay out additional funds to cover its guarantee of HOLC bonds.

This story, however, does not carefully account for the costs borne by the Treasury on behalf of the HOLC but not reported by the HOLC in its final report in 1952. HOLC accounting reports took a narrow view of its costs and revenues, without thinking too much about alternative uses of its funds elsewhere in the government, or about costs borne by other agencies to support HOLC operations. In contrast, the Comptroller General thought more about the net costs of the program from the entire government's, and thus the taxpayers', perspective. One item that the Comptroller General identifies is the time cost of money. The Treasury was not willing to give out $200 million to just anyone who in twenty years could repay the $200 million. That is bad business, even for a government agency, and no bank would be willing to make such a loan. If the Treasury did not care about inflation, it could have just held onto the cash with no risk. On the basis of inflation alone, $1 in 1934 was the equivalent of $1.94 in 1952, implying that the HOLC would have had to pay back $388 million in 1951 to break even on the investment in real (inflation-adjusted) terms.[4] At the very least, the federal government could have chosen to pay down the federal debt by $200 million in 1933 and avoid nearly twenty years' worth of interest payments. Alternatively, it could have used the money to fund any of the many other Depression-era programs designed to bolster the economy. The Comptroller General estimated that the cost for supplying funds to the corporation was $91.9 million, which had not been listed in the HOLC final report. Mainly these costs consisted of interest paid to holders of the $200 million in bonds the Treasury had issued to fund its initial investment in the HOLC.[5]

The Comptroller General was also careful to take into account the fact that the HOLC actually ran three programs. In this book, we generally discuss only the HOLC's loan-refinancing program. However, the HOLC also invested $100 million in the Federal Savings and Loan Insurance Corporation and $223.9 million in federal and state savings and loan associations.

In order to understand the profitability of the loan purchase and refinance program, we also need to separate out the latter two operations. Furthermore, when considering the mortgage program, we need to take into account not just the $200 million initial investment by the Treasury, but also the ongoing subsidy provided by the federal government's guarantee of the $3.09 billion in HOLC bonds.

Table 10.1 uses information from the Comptroller General's report to show the cumulative income and cost to the federal government at the end of the program. It does not use the standard business methods of discounting to obtain the net present value. Instead, it simply adds up the costs and expenses over time to come to an accumulated amount at the end of the period.

The income and expenses for the HOLC loan purchase and refinance program at the top of table 10.1 show that the HOLC received cumulative interest payments of around $1.2 billion from its borrowers and had a net profit on its rental and sale of foreclosed properties of $25.8 million. The HOLC paid $598 million in interest on bonds that supported the loan and refinance program. Additional interest costs covered by the US Treasury were about $83 million (part of the $91.9 million cost of supplying funds noted above). The HOLC also had administrative and operating expenses of around $263 million over the life of the program. In addition, it had losses on loans and insurance-related issues of about $338 million. Altogether, after subtracting $1.282 billion in total expenses from the $1.229 billion in total income, it is apparent that the HOLC loan program lost about $53 million. This is about 1.8 percent of the value of the loans it refinanced, roughly $53 per loan.

Now we have the facts—the HOLC lost about $53 million to the government while refinancing about $3 billion worth of loans. While this indicates the program was not profitable, as is often claimed, it clearly was also not a large source of loss to the federal government.

Foreclosures were a main source of the HOLC's expenses and were the most significant expense item that was not really under the HOLC's control. With such expenses amounting to about $337 million, the implied loss was about 33 percent on average across all of the roughly 200,000 foreclosed properties. Since most of these foreclosures took place in the late 1930s before the economic expansion of the next decade, the HOLC's finances were particularly bleak in that period. Had the HOLC been evaluated in 1938 based on current *mark-to-market* accounting standards for financial institutions,

**Table 10.1. Net costs to the federal government of HOLC programs**

*Loan program*

| | |
|---|---:|
| Income | $1,229,560,289 |
| Interest on loans and related advances | $1,192,016,623 |
| Net income from property operation | $25,818,935 |
| Premiums on sales of loan accounts | $2,241,649 |
| Miscellaneous | $9,483,082 |
| Expenses | $1,282,857,703 |
| Interest and other financing expenses within the HOLC | $598,120,287 |
| Interest expenses covered by US Treasury | $83,190,679 |
| Administrative and operating expenses | $263,539,744 |
| Losses: loans and related transactions | $337,154,236 |
| Losses: fidelity and casualty | $372,053 |
| Losses: fire and other hazards | $367,536 |
| Losses: other | $113,168 |
| Net income | −$53,297,414 |

*Other programs*

| | |
|---|---:|
| Income | $74,380,282 |
| Dividends and interest on investments in savings and loan associations | $44,745,479 |
| Dividends on investment in Federal Savings and Loan Insurance Corporation | $28,217,076 |
| Interest on investments in government securities | $1,417,727 |
| Expenses | $98,917,426 |
| Interest and other financing expenses within the HOLC | $62,617,849 |
| Interest expenses covered by US Treasury | $8,709,321 |
| Administrative and operating expenses | $27,590,256 |
| Net income from other programs | −$24,537,144 |

*Sources*: Comptroller General of the United States (1953, 9, 27–28); Federal Home Loan Bank Administration (1952, 3, 4, 15).

*Notes:* The HOLC final report and the Comptroller General's audit did not separate out some of the costs for the loan program, the investment in the Federal Savings and Loan Insurance Corporation, or the investments in savings and loan associations. We prorated the costs based on the proportions of the investments listed in the HOLC final report. The HOLC sold $3.09 billion in bonds to finance the loan program. It also invested $100 million in the Federal Savings and Loan Insurance Corporation and $223.9 million in federal and state savings and loan associations. Thus, the proportion of the interest costs and operating costs assigned to the loan program was 0.9052, and the rest was assigned to the investments in the Federal Savings and Loan Insurance Corporation and the savings and loan associations.

which require firms to evaluate their assets at the resale prices of the assets, it is very likely that the HOLC would have been considered insolvent in the late 1930s. However, economic fortunes changed in the very late 1930s and 1940s, the Mead-Barry Act liberalized loan terms for HOLC borrowers in 1939, and the HOLC's loan portfolio improved enough to deliver the financial results reviewed above.

The discussion has focused on the HOLC loan purchase and loan refinancing program because that is the focus of this book and because it would only muddy the waters to evaluate the costs of that program combined with the HOLC's investments in the Federal Savings and Loan Insurance Corporation and in savings and loans. The income and expenses for those investments, at the bottom of table 10.1, show that the HOLC lost about $24.5 million on those operations after taking into account the two programs' shares of the Treasury costs of supplying funds.

## The Size of the Subsidy from the Government Program

Because the HOLC purchased about $3 billion worth of mortgages, the $200 million capitalization from the Treasury was not nearly enough to finance more than a small portion of its activity. We have focused so far on whether that initial investment of $200 million was profitable, but there is also the larger question of the risk to which taxpayers were exposed through the other $2.8 billion of funds. These funds came to the HOLC via bond issuance, and since the bonds were guaranteed by the federal government, taxpayers were potentially on the hook to repay them. This guarantee was in effect a subsidy given to lenders and borrowers through the HOLC's loan purchase and refinance program.

In financing the loan program, the HOLC had a major advantage over any private firm that tried to run such a program because the federal government and American taxpayers were backing the HOLC bonds. One way of observing the importance of the federal guarantee is by noting the change in interest rates on HOLC bonds during its first two years of operation. On the original HOLC bonds issued in 1933, the government guaranteed the interest but not the principal. This essentially created a firewall to protect taxpayers. The principal of the bonds was backed by the underlying mortgages and nothing else. If enough of the loans defaulted in that initial arrangement, there might not have been enough revenue to pay the bonds in full. In compensation for that risk, the HOLC offered a 4 percent interest rate on the original bond issue. In comparison, high-grade corporate bonds of similar length were paying 4.11 percent.[6]

The riskiness of its initial bonds proved problematic in the early days of the HOLC. As noted in chapter 6, the first bond issues in 1933 were reportedly treated with some skepticism by the market, and they traded for prices as low as 80–85 cents on the dollar. This complicated the HOLC's loan purchase activities, as lenders were reluctant to take on bonds, given the risk and uncertainty. When the HOLC was transacting with the lenders, it wanted the lenders to treat the bonds as worth their face value rather than the value at which the bonds were trading, but some lenders balked. This was enough of a discount to make lender participation a bit more difficult to obtain, but it was not a crippling problem. Representative Thomas Busby from Mississippi noted that the bonds "were not good to the financial investors because they did not have Uncle Sam's Guarantee."[7] President Roosevelt weighed in as well, asserting a "moral obligation in respect to these bonds."[8]

As a result, in April 1934 Congress and the president enacted legislation that guaranteed the principal on HOLC bonds as well. This meant that HOLC bonds were de facto equivalent to US Treasury securities, the only effective difference being that a specific revenue stream from the HOLC would be devoted to repaying them. In fact, the act creating the HOLC required that principal payments on HOLC mortgages be solely used to retire HOLC bonds, a requirement that helped ensure that the HOLC would eventually close down rather than become an open-ended government program. When the HOLC issued its new A series bonds in May 1934, the interest rate was 3 percent, nearly a percentage point below the 3.91 rate for high-grade corporate bonds. From that point forward, HOLC bonds were generally issued at rates that were from 0.6 to 1 percent lower than for high-grade corporate bonds of longer than one year. The HOLC also issued some one-year bonds that carried interest rates about 0.2 percentage points lower than one-year rates on high-grade corporate bonds.[9]

In making calculations the way the Comptroller General made them for the HOLC, a 1 percent increase in the interest rate for the loan program would have increased its costs by roughly $300 million, increasing its net loss from $53 million to $353 million. The new cost would have been about $353 per loan, or 12 percent of the total loan value. A discussion from chapter 5 is relevant here, regarding whether a privately financed bad bank would have been a realistic alternative to the HOLC. A privately financed bad bank that matched the HOLC's foreclosure experience—foreclosing on 20 percent of its loans at a loss of 30 percent on each loan—would likely have been required by investors to pay interest rates on its bonds at least 1 percent higher in compensation for the risk. Interest rates would have been 2 percent higher if a foreclosure share of 30 percent had been anticipated. Thus a bad bank seeking capital from private bond markets might have faced interest rates that were higher by 2 percent or more than the risk-free government rate. Had the interest rate on private bad bank bonds been 2 percent higher than on the HOLC bonds, the subsidy would have risen to roughly $653 million, or 22 percent of the value of the HOLC loans made.

Fortunately for the taxpayers, the federal government never had to come through with the guarantee of HOLC bonds. The interest and principal on the bonds were eventually paid off from interest and principal payments on the loan portfolio, rental and sales revenue from foreclosed properties, and revenue from the HOLC's other programs. Two forces were probably most responsible for the relative financial success of the HOLC. One was the ability to borrow cheaply on the bond market, given the federal government's guarantee of its bonds. The other force was the economic recovery of the late 1930s and early 1940s, along with the economic environment of World War II, which raised housing prices and incomes, greatly stemming the tide of foreclosures that had persisted into the late 1930s. As one observer of the HOLC noted, "The war boom fortunately intervened to save HOLC from embarrassment and converted a speculation into an ostensibly costless investment."[10]

# CHAPTER 11

# CONCLUSION

The Roosevelt administration and Democratic Congress created the HOLC in 1933 in response to a relentless foreclosure crisis that threatened large numbers of home owners and appeared to be getting much worse. When Franklin Roosevelt proposed the HOLC to Congress in 1933, he asked legislators to take the historic step of creating a new role for the federal government in dealing with the housing industry: "The broad interests of the nation require that special safeguards should be thrown around home ownership as a guaranty of social and economic stability, and that to protect home owners from inequitable enforced liquidation, in a time of general distress, is a proper concern of the Government."

To achieve these ends, the legislation called for the creation of a government-sponsored corporation that issued bonds to purchase and refinance mortgage loans. The goals of the HOLC were to help lenders by removing toxic assets from their books and to assist borrowers in trouble through no fault of their own, while minimizing losses for the taxpayer.

How the HOLC fared can be summarized broadly in four statements. First, the HOLC was effective in purchasing a large number of distressed loans from lenders because it offered them a good bargain. Second, the HOLC delivered relief to borrowers by liberalizing loan terms and servicing these loans patiently, but the HOLC typically did not provide significant reductions in the principal owed. Third, the HOLC's purchases and refinancing of loans helped stave off damage from the foreclosure crisis of the 1930s but could not reverse all of its impacts. Finally, close examination of the HOLC's finances suggests that the HOLC had losses on its government accounts of about 2 percent of the value of loans made, while the subsidy to home owners and lenders might have ranged as high as 12 to 22 percent.

Given the recent mortgage boom and crisis, an obvious question is whether a modern HOLC would work well today. It is clear that a new HOLC could not operate in the same way that it did in the 1930s because of the substantial differences between the structures of loans and mortgage markets in the early 1930s and the current era. Modern structures have evolved from foundations set by the HOLC and other New Deal housing policies. The evolution has altered some of the constraints under which borrowers and lenders operate today. However, it has not altered the basic economic forces present in all mortgage markets that shape how we should think about an economic intervention like the HOLC. In general, the challenge of loan modification or refinance programs in any era is to strike a balance across three sometimes conflicting goals—to secure lender participation, to provide borrowers with relief, and to not break the public's bank in the process. In performing these functions, the historical HOLC can be seen as setting a template for one particular type of intervention, a modern bad bank that issues bonds guaranteed by the government to purchase and finance distressed loans from private lenders.

We provide context for the discussion of our four principal results by first pointing out important long-term changes in the institutional structure of mortgage and housing markets since the 1930s that made a difference in how the HOLC was structured and how it operated. In discussing the results, we also illustrate fundamental issues involved in loan modification programs by comparing the HOLC program to the two largest federal programs that have been implemented during the recent mortgage crisis. We close with a discussion of how the experience of the HOLC sets expectations for current and future mortgage modification programs.

## Changes in the Institutional Environment
The HOLC was a product of its time. When the Roosevelt administration and Democratic Congress introduced the HOLC in 1933, they started with a blank slate, given that there had been little prior federal involvement with residential mortgage markets. Fewer than 45 percent of nonfarm households owned

their homes at the time, and the foreclosure crisis was revealing the short-comings of the traditional types of contracts (short-term, interest-only, and share-accumulation B&L loans) that were popular in the mortgage market. On the other hand, borrowers had substantial equity in their homes when these loans were made in the 1920s because loan-to-value ratios on first mortgages were generally at most 60 percent. The relatively low level of indebtedness among borrowers provided plenty of room for the HOLC to aid borrowers by adjusting the terms of repayment without cutting the principal owed on the loans. Thus, the HOLC was in a position where it could purchase troubled loans from lenders at near full value and still do a great deal to improve the terms of the mortgage for borrowers.

The experiences of the 1930s led to numerous changes in nonfarm mortgage markets that set the institutional environment for the crisis in the early 2000s. Since World War II the typical home mortgage loan in the United States has been structured much like HOLC loans, although with even higher loan-to-value ratios and longer periods for repayment. But unlike in the 1930s, the federal government was already involved in housing finance in several ways before the mortgage crisis of 2007, including through Federal Housing Administration and Veterans Administration loan insurance, and the implicit guarantees behind Fannie Mae and Freddie Mac. These and other subsidies had been supported for decades by both Democratic and Republican policy makers to expand home ownership in the United States. As a result, legislators in 2007 did not have the luxury of facing the kind of blank slate that existed in 1933 when a mortgage crisis could be ameliorated simply by providing access to loans with fifteen-year maturities, 80 percent loan-to-value ratios, and lower-than-prevailing private-market interest rates.

Within the modern environment, the federal government has deployed several programs to aid lenders and home owners involved in the mortgage crisis of the early 2000s. The most prominent among these, the Home Affordable Modification Program (HAMP) and Hope for Home Owners (H4H), have focused, as did the HOLC, on modifying distressed loans. In addition, the Treasury, Federal Deposit Insurance Corporation, and Federal Reserve have taken other extraordinary steps to prevent financial markets and institutions from failing. These activities include taking ownership stakes in large banks, as the Reconstruction Finance Corporation had in the 1930s, but also bailing out Fannie Mae, Freddie Mac, and AIG, the largest insurer in the world. A broad comparison of the impacts of all of the programs implemented during the mortgage crises of the 1930s and the early 2000s is beyond the scope of this book, but they certainly shape the context in which the loan modification programs operated.

## Attracting the Participation of Lenders

Lender participation was a major design constraint for the HOLC during the 1930s and remains a major constraint today for any government-led modification program. HOLC officials deliberately offered lenders good bargains to make sure that they could refinance a large share of loans for deserving borrowers whom they thought could successfully repay modified loans. Lenders received HOLC bonds that were valued at or near the full debts owed to them, including principal and interest, and any insurance or property tax payments they had made on behalf of borrowers. Moreover, because some lenders balked at accepting the initial bonds that carried federal guarantee of interest only, within a year the HOLC was given the ability to issue new bonds that were fully guaranteed. Altogether, the HOLC replaced the risky mortgages on lenders' books with safe and liquid bonds.

Today, the HOLC approach of purchasing loans directly from lenders would be substantially more complicated than it was during the 1930s, partly because of the much higher prevalence of securitization. The fragmented ownership that results from securitization creates difficulties in purchasing loans that do not arise when a loan has a single owner. These complications help explain why neither of the two main modification programs put in place by the federal government beginning in 2008 was designed to replicate the HOLC's model of whole-loan purchases.[1] The different structures of these programs, however, should not distract us from the fact that obtaining lender participation is a difficult problem today, just as it was in the 1930s. Broadly speaking, the calculus of lender participation remains largely the same. Lenders negotiate with the government over each mortgage and then decide whether to accept the government's offer to participate.

The first major modern modification program in recent years, H4H, was created under the Bush administration. Like any modification program, participating in H4H presented both benefits and costs to lenders. H4H was designed mainly as a debt reduction program and asked lenders to reduce eligible borrowers' debts to 96.5 percent of market value. For first-lien holders, this cost of participation was meant to be balanced by the availability of insurance against redefault on their new modified loans through the Federal Housing Administration. Some direct payments were also eventually available for second-lien holders as an incentive to extinguish their claims.[2]

The second major modification program in recent years is HAMP, created under the Obama administration. HAMP focuses on the affordability of monthly payments for borrowers rather than on the total amount of debt relative to property values. The program's magic number is thirty-one, the target maximum for the borrowers' monthly payments as a percentage of their monthly incomes. HAMP meets this target in three successive steps, first by lowering the interest rate, then (if necessary) by extending the length of the loan, and finally (if necessary) by leaving some principal to be paid as a lump sum at the end of the loan rather than month by month. The incentive for lenders' participation is mainly a set of direct payments from the Treasury to loan servicers and investors.[3]

Lender participation was a critical constraint in limiting the number of modifications through H4H, which reached fewer than 600 borrowers even though it was designed and funded to reach about 400,000.[4] The carrot of FHA insurance was evidently not enough to convince lenders to grant debt reductions as the program required. HAMP's design was in part a response to the problems with lender participation in the H4H program. HAMP has worked to make modifications attractive to the owners and servicers of loans by adding payments designed to make the net present value of the flow of payments under the HAMP modification exceed the net present value of the lender's *expected* flow of payments from staying with the original loan. Nevertheless, the number of HAMP modifications has been considered a disappointment because its 1.1 million permanent modifications through April 2011 have fallen well short of the 3 or 4 million originally anticipated. HAMP has reached about 1.5 percent of nonfarm homes, a much smaller percentage of home owners than the 10 percent reached by the HOLC.[5]

There are several reasons why the HAMP has reached a smaller share of home owners than the HOLC did. One reason is that the math of HAMP participation requires finding a way to deliver relief to borrowers without principal reductions, even as many already had loans with high loan-to-value ratios and generous repayment terms by historical standards. HAMP has less leeway to provide better terms for borrowers than the HOLC, barring principal reductions. In general we suspect that the HAMP subsidies in the loan refinancing do not compensate lenders to the same extent the HOLC loan purchases did, but a careful study needs to be performed to document this claim.

In considering lender participation with the HOLC, it is important to realize that it was not inevitable that the HOLC would secure the participation of such a large share of lenders and borrowers. HOLC officials made deliberate choices to achieve liftoff by offering lenders prices for their loans that were close to the full value of the debts. Today, a similarly deliberate effort would be needed to build a program to the same size as the HOLC. Putting aside the benefits to borrowers or the housing market, the benefit of such a policy to lenders would likely be different than in the 1930s and a bit unclear. In the 2000s the federal government has already assumed substantial risks in mortgage markets by bailing out Freddie Mac and Fannie Mae. This has ensured a continuous supply of funds for new loans (as long as those loans conform to the standards for Fannie and Freddie, an important if), which was lacking in the 1930s. Further, generous payments to lenders could set precedents for future bailouts that, in turn, would create incentives for lenders and borrowers to take more risk because they believe the government would act again to save them in a future crisis. However, we are not aware of any evidence that the HOLC set such a precedent in the decades following its liquidation.

## Providing Relief for Borrowers

In both the 1930s and 2000–2010, home foreclosure crises developed when borrowers faced a combination of declining incomes and declining home prices. In the 1920s, when future HOLC borrowers took out their original loans, the borrowers would have been considered prime borrowers based on modern credit standards. However, when they tried to refinance their loans during the foreclosure crisis of the early 1930s, they were typically in deep trouble. They had few resources available to repay the principal on their loans. Further, many had lost jobs or seen their hours cut sharply, so they no longer were good prospects for refinanced loans. Meanwhile, home prices also fell by 20 to 40 percent, cutting into home owners' equity. In a significant majority of cases, the home owners did not owe more than the value of their homes because the loan-to-value ratios of HOLC borrowers were generally limited to 50 to 60 percent on a first mortgage, and 80 percent on two mortgages combined. However, the value of a home was difficult to define in a dysfunctional housing market in which borrowers could not easily obtain refinancing and buyers could not easily get credit. This combination of declines in income, housing values, and lender assets led to a large number of foreclosures even though many borrowers did not owe lenders more than the value of their homes.

The Great Recession of 2007 was not nearly as severe as the Great Depression, yet declining incomes and housing prices also have played major roles in the recent foreclosure crisis. Two-thirds of HAMP participants have experienced job loss or income cuts. Meanwhile, declining home prices left many borrowers underwater because the loan-to-value ratios for modern mortgages at the time of origination typically ranged from 80 to 100 percent.

When the HOLC refinanced loans, relief for HOLC borrowers came primarily from a variety of devices that lowered monthly payments, including delayed payment on the principal until June 1936, lower interest rates, and longer loan durations. The HOLC arranged for some debt forgiveness, but borrowers' HOLC loans totaled more than 90 percent of their prior debts on average, and debt reductions were often related to accrued interest rather than principal. The HOLC had no specific target for monthly payments relative to borrowers' incomes. The modern HAMP program does have such a target and has followed a similar strategy of lowering interest rates, lengthening loan duration, and delaying principal payments. Even more than the HOLC, very few HAMP modifications have taken an additional step of reducing the principal on the loans, although a separate small program involving principal reductions has been established.[6] The HOLC, however, had more room to improve the terms of the loan without such reductions because the original loans in the 1930s started with shorter loan durations, higher loan-to-value ratios, and higher interest rates before modification.

When employment prospects remained weak late into the 1930s, the HOLC delivered more relief by lowering the interest rate on its loans and allowing loan durations to be extended to twenty-five years. These liberalizations, along with economic growth in the 1940s, helped cure a large part of the HOLC's significant problem with delinquent borrowers.

The HOLC also delivered relief to its borrowers through its servicing practices. The HOLC generally delayed foreclosures on delinquent loans while trying to determine whether there was some chance the borrower could repay if given more time. The HOLC's service agents in a number of cases took the process a step further and tried to help home owners find jobs and resources with which to repay their loans. In the process the HOLC also sought to take into account the impact of additional foreclosures on housing markets. After taking possession of properties on which it foreclosed, the HOLC repaired the homes, rented them out, and tried to time the sale of the homes to avoid lowering housing prices within local markets.

Servicing loans has become an important issue in the modern era as well. The HOLC directly acquired the servicing rights, as they were typically not unbundled from loan ownership during the 1930s. While modern programs have avoided replicating the HOLC's strategy of purchasing whole loans, it would be possible for a modern program to purchase only the servicing rights on them. Nevertheless, no modern program has attempted this, as far as we know, perhaps because the HOLC's track record as a loan servicer is not widely known.

While HAMP has not involved direct government servicing of modified loans, the program was designed to address servicer incentives by providing direct payments in a "pay-for-success" approach to modification. Nevertheless, there have been many difficulties with the post-modification servicing of HAMP loans, including the suspension of two of the nation's largest servicers due to poor performance. Fundamentally, most servicing contracts today do little to encourage servicers to pursue modifications or ensure the success of modified loans, and HAMP leaves those contracts intact. For example, servicers often receive fees for executing foreclosures but receive nothing for doing detailed case work for a modification, and are often required to cover any missed payments. In general, the modern servicing industry has been designed for routine tasks like payment processing, resulting in a lean structure that has trouble with the inherently labor-intensive process of modifying loans. Federal regulators have stated that servicers "misapply payments, lose paperwork, file incorrect foreclosure affidavits, or simply do not answer the phone or make available knowledgeable staff persons."[7] The recent "robo-signing" scandal is symptomatic of these problems. We do not yet know the contribution that servicer behavior will make to reducing the number of foreclosures within the HAMP program, but we expect it to be less important than in the HOLC, based simply on the differences in the structure of the two programs.

## The HOLC's Impact on Housing and Mortgage Markets

The 1930s were a disastrous decade for housing and mortgage markets. On a national basis, foreclosures were still elevated for most of the 1930s, and the HOLC itself foreclosed on 19 percent of its loans. The decade between

1930 and 1940 recorded the only decrease in the nonfarm home-ownership rate during the twentieth century, from 45 to 40 percent. In addition, over the decade nominal home values decreased by nearly 40 percent, and housing construction remained well below 1920s levels.

The HOLC was able to repair some of the damage from the foreclosure crisis by preventing even greater declines in housing values and home-ownership rates in many communities. In a typical small community, HOLC spending staved off about a 16 percent decline in the value of homes and kept about 11 percent more home owners in their homes. The impact on larger communities with over fifty thousand people is more difficult to parse statistically and remains unclear at this point.

The HOLC's repair of the damage without promoting full recovery underscores the limitations of policy in counteracting the powerful forces of an economic downturn. After all, the HOLC was a massive program, and our research indicates it distributed its loans to areas in a pattern that reflected the severity of housing market distress, rather than the need for general relief or political considerations. Altogether, the HOLC refinanced about 20 percent of the nation's nonfarm residential real estate loans from 1933 to 1936. If another HOLC existed today, it would have to refinance roughly $2 trillion of loans to replicate that record. Thus, if any program could be a panacea for a mortgage crisis due to size and distribution alone, the HOLC would be that program. The fact that it was not tells us just how large the problems were in the housing market at the time.

Even when successful, policies like the HOLC do no more than remove a potentially important impediment to the adjustment process. At the time, there were no mortgage guarantees from the Federal Housing Administration, Veterans Administration, Fannie Mae, or Freddie Mac that protected the owners of loans or securities from the risk of default, and lenders did not have the protections of the liability insurance provided by agencies like the Federal Deposit Insurance Corporation. In the absence of such guarantees, the financial accelerator was more powerful than it is today. In turn, this increased the value and impact of an intervention like the HOLC.

## HOLC Finances

Close examination of HOLC finances suggests that the program lost about $53 million in the government accounts from its loan-refinancing operations, which came to about 2 percent of the value of the loans made. This performance was much better than forecasted by skeptics when the program was created, but disputes the perception in modern commentary that the HOLC actually made a small profit. In looking back on the actual course of history, it is easy to forget the uncertainty that existed in 1933 about how much the HOLC would cost, and to underappreciate the risks borne by taxpayers who guaranteed the HOLC's bonds. Counterfactual history can be a dubious exercise, but is useful in challenging the natural tendency to view past events as deterministic rather than the result of various historical contingencies. When the HOLC began operations, observers had only broad notions of how much the program would cost, and few were confident they knew how large a program the HOLC would actually be. Some of the key contingencies that buoyed the HOLC's finances include the economic expansion of the late 1930s and 1940s, as well as the effect of World War II on property values.

Another key turning point in the HOLC's finances was the guarantee of its bonds. We have noted that at first many lenders balked at accepting HOLC bonds, which initially bore the federal government's guarantee only on their interest payments. Congress and the president could have taken a hard line and refused to change the financial design, but they instead chose to fully guarantee the bonds in 1934. This concession is worth repeating because it had profound implications for the allocation of the program's financial risk. Had the HOLC financed its program without the guarantee, the interest rates on its bonds would likely have been at least 1, and possibly up to 3, percentage points higher. A 1 percentage point increase in the interest rate on HOLC bonds would have added approximately $300 million to the HOLC's costs, or roughly 10 percent of the value of the $3 billion in loans made. Thus, the subsidy provided to mortgage markets by the HOLC's activity likely would have been at least 12 percent of the value of the loans made. Each additional 1 percentage point rise would have raised the subsidy by another 10 percent of the value of the loans.

To put the HOLC's risks and costs into perspective, it is useful to review how the federal government has supported Fannie Mae and Freddie Mac starting in September 2008. Both companies, which buy and securitize a large portion of US residential mortgage loans, were privately held before the recent crisis but had implicit public support. That support was made explicit in September 2008 when the federal government began recapitalizing the two companies.

By the middle of 2012, the Treasury had invested roughly $185 billion, over 1 percent of GDP, in preferred stock of the two enterprises, but the ultimate losses associated with the government backstop could be significantly lower or higher than that number.[8] The scale of the amounts invested in Fannie and Freddie demonstrate the risk taken on by the HOLC in the mid-1930s when it purchased and refinanced troubled mortgage loans that were equal to approximately 4 percent of GDP.[9] The risks associated with the investment were also greater because the HOLC specialized in distressed loans, whereas Fannie and Freddie own or guarantee a large number of loans that have shown no sign of trouble so far.

The HOLC ran risks because it owned loans, and therefore was exposed to potential losses from foreclosure. In contrast, the most significant modern loan modification program, HAMP, has avoided ownership of loans. Instead, it has given lenders incentives to renegotiate loans with their borrowers; therefore, HAMP and taxpayers are not taking direct risks. Though H4H entailed risks for taxpayers through insuring modified loans against redefault, this has ultimately been a moot risk for taxpayers since so few lenders and borrowers availed themselves of the program.

The narrow focus on the HOLC's costs should also not overshadow the more important fact that programs like the HOLC are conceived because mortgage crises themselves are very costly to society. Even though the subsidy provided to home owners and lenders by the HOLC might have been as high as 22 percent of the value of the loans, the benefits that came from staving off foreclosures and preventing further declines in home values may well have more than covered the size of the subsidy.

### Setting Expectations for Mortgage Resolution Policies

The HOLC experience offers an important lesson for setting expectations about any public policy that is implemented to resolve a mortgage crisis. These crises tend to be lengthy, difficult, and costly to resolve because homes are long-term durable goods, mortgages are long-term financial assets, and financial crises typically lead to longer economic downturns, which can feed back into the financial crises. The mechanism is familiar. It takes time for home owners to default, and for lenders to foreclose, after housing prices, employment, and household income begin to fall. When the number of foreclosures finally rises, the downward pressure on housing prices is intensified and causes additional deterioration in the balance sheets of home owners and mortgage lenders. Mortgage resolution programs are implemented at this point so that these latter shocks do not shut down housing and mortgage markets and thereby lengthen and deepen the original distress within them.

The nation was six years past the peak of a building boom, three years into a general foreclosure crisis, and had seen housing prices fall by nearly a third when the HOLC was established in 1933. By that time distress was so widespread that more than twenty states had imposed some form of moratorium to delay additional foreclosures that threatened more than one-fifth of home owners and nearly every mortgage lender. The HOLC was created in response to this environment and prevented hundreds of thousands from losing their homes while helping to prop up housing prices. Despite these successes, the HOLC still ran into its share of problems. By 1941 the HOLC had foreclosed on nearly one-fifth of its own loans and was still dealing with many delinquent borrowers. The HOLC experience suggests that in nearly every setting, any modification process will likely be a lengthy and painful process involving a significant number of reversals of fortune for those involved.

# APPENDIX
## Walking through the Analysis of the Impact of the HOLC

For the interested reader, we walk through the analysis that led to the numbers on the HOLC's impact on housing markets discussed in chapter 9. This appendix also shows how the results change as the analysis starts with the simplest comparisons and then takes into account more and more issues that would influence the final results. The appendix is designed to show the thought processes that go into a careful statistical analysis and to show why the simplest comparisons can be misleading.

One note before continuing: The HOLC program focused on nonfarm homes because there was an alternative program for farm owners through the Farm Credit Administration. Throughout this appendix, therefore, every time home owners and housing values are mentioned, they refer to nonfarm owners and nonfarm housing values.

### The Simplest Analysis
The simplest, but flawed, analysis can be shown by plotting relationships on some graphs. Figure A.1 plots the relationship between the value of owned non-farm homes in 1940 and the value of per capita HOLC loans distributed between 1933 and 1936 for the nearly 2,500 counties with fewer than fifty thousand people. Counties with fewer than fifty thousand people accounted for 87 percent of all counties and 39 percent of the population at the time. The focus is on this group of counties because the research teams found that the HOLC was most successful in smaller counties. Discussion of the larger counties will follow.

Figure A.1 does not show much. If you squint, the huge mass of points with stray dots spraying out somewhat upward to the right might look like a group of bees leaving a hive. The line on the graph best captures the simple average relationship between the HOLC loans and the housing values, but from the wide scattering of points around the line, clearly this relationship is not too strong. The slope of the line tells us that $1 in annual HOLC loans per capita increased the value of the home by $160. Since the typical median value of homes in these counties was about $1,431 in 1940, the $160 increase is an increase of 11.2 percent. The median value of $1,431 may not seem like much money to modern readers, but it was roughly double the average annual earnings of manufacturing workers in these small counties in 1939. Housing prices had fallen sharply since 1930, when they were roughly 3.3 times the average earnings of manufacturing workers in counties of this size. Around the year 2000, the median housing values nationwide were about seven or eight times average annual earnings for manufacturing workers.

The reason that a large number of points on the graph in figure A.1 do not fit the line is because the HOLC was not the only factor underlying house prices. A large number of other factors also determine housing values in each city. They include incomes, interest rates on loans, geographic features of the cities, the demographic features of the population, the effects of other federal and state programs, the housing prices earlier in the decade, and prior trends in housing prices in the 1920s. Many of these factors varied a great deal across cities. The results after controlling for differences across cities in these factors are shown below.

If we do the same exercise, except we look at the number of nonfarm home owners instead of house prices, we find another very loose relationship,

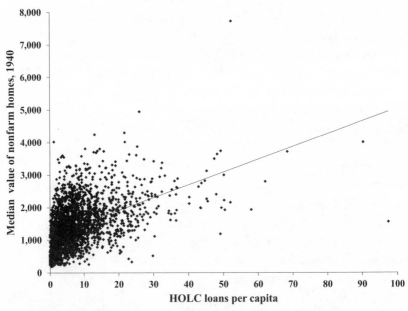

**Figure A.1.** HOLC activity and home values in 1940, by county. Counties with fewer than fifty thousand people. Self-reported values. (Data from Federal Home Loan Bank Board 1938a and US Census 1933, 1943.)

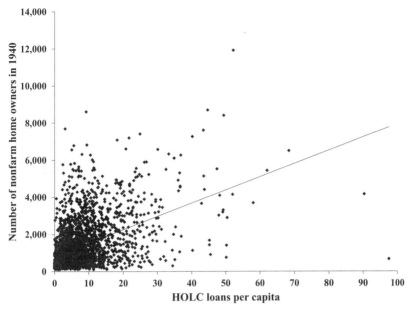

**Figure A.2.** *HOLC activity and number of home owners in 1940, by county. Counties with fewer than fifty thousand people. (Data from Federal Home Loan Bank Board 1938a and US Census 1933, 1943.)*

displayed in figure A.2, again for counties with less than fifty thousand people. The line that shows the simplest relationship between the HOLC loans per capita and the number of home owners suggests that an additional dollar of annual HOLC loans per capita would have increased the number of home owners by 295, which implies a rise of about 21 percent from the average of 1,406 in 1930. The number of nonfarm home owners in these counties seems small, but remember that most counties with fewer than fifty thousand people had a large number of farmers, who were not eligible for HOLC loans.

## One Step Forward: Controlling for Initial Conditions in 1930
Both graphs suggest that the HOLC must have been very successful, because both housing values and the number of home owners in 1940 were substantially larger in areas with more HOLC loans per capita. Yet a great deal of care should be taken before accepting these figures at face value. Many of the counties with higher housing values in 1940 also had higher values in 1930 before the HOLC ever existed. For example, borrowers in Reno, Nevada, re-

ceived HOLC loans of $90.30 per capita, and median home values there in 1940 were $4,007. Both were among the highest values in the country. At the other end of the scale, borrowers in Monticello, Mississippi, received only $1.29 in HOLC funds per capita, and median home values in 1940 were only $911. If we focused only on this information, it seems as though we would attribute a large effect to the HOLC.

However, the large gap in home values was already there before the HOLC ever existed. The average Reno home in 1930 was valued at $5,013 compared to only $1,081 in Monticello. In fact, a graph comparing 1930 housing values to the value of HOLC loans per capita for all counties under fifty thousand people looks a great deal like figure A.1. Similarly, a graph comparing the number of home owners in 1930 with the value of HOLC loans per capita looks quite similar to figure A.2.

Therefore, it is important to take into account what the housing values looked like in 1930 when examining the relationship between the HOLC and housing values. One way to do this is to look at the relationship between the *change* in housing values between 1930 and 1940 and the *change* in HOLC loans per capita between the 1930s and 1920s. Since there were no HOLC loans in the 1920s, the change in HOLC loans per capita between the 1920s and 1930s is the same as the 1930s value of the HOLC loans per capita.

By looking at the changes, the analysis controls for a broad range of factors that did not change in the 1930s but would have influenced housing values and home ownership. The factors included things like climate, local building codes, locations of cities near rivers and coast lines, housing regulations, and infrastructure. Figure A.3 shows the relationship between the *change* in median home values between 1930 and 1940 and the value of HOLC loans per capita in the 1930s. Note the quite different shapes in figures A.3 and A.1. The line in figure A.3 suggests that housing values *fell* by $75 more in counties with an extra dollar of HOLC loans per capita. In contrast, the positive slope of the line in figure A.1 implied a *rise* of $160 for an extra dollar of HOLC loans per capita. These results are at odds, but we are not done with the analysis quite yet.

The plot of the change in the number of home owners from 1930 to 1940 against HOLC loans per capita in figure A.4 suggests a weak relationship between HOLC loans per capita and the change in the number of home owners. The line in figure A.4 shows that another dollar in HOLC spending per capita

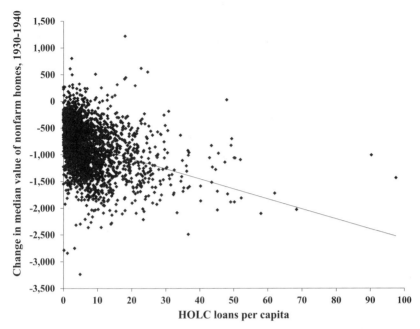

**Figure A.3.** *HOLC activity and the change in home values, 1930–1940, by county. Counties with fewer than fifty thousand people. Self-reported values. (Data from Federal Home Loan Bank Board 1938a and US Census 1933, 1943.)*

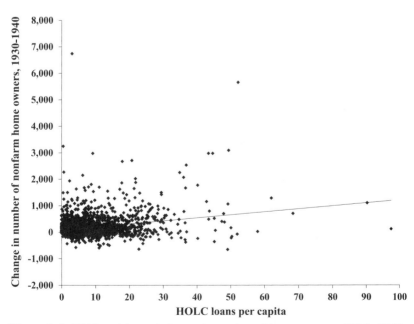

**Figure A.4.** *HOLC activity and change in number of home owners, 1930–1940, by county. Counties with fewer than fifty thousand people. (Data from Federal Home Loan Bank Board 1938a and US Census 1933, 1943.)*

raised the change in nonfarm home owners by 45 households. This is a much weaker relationship than the 295-household increase suggested by the data in figure A.2.

**Two Steps Forward: Accounting for Other Community Characteristics**

The introduction of the HOLC was not the only factor changing over the course of the 1930s. The New Deal introduced relief programs, public works programs, and farm programs. The economy in some counties fared better than in other counties. The changes in age structure, income distribution, education, and racial and ethnic features of the population also differed substantially across counties. The trends in housing values and home-ownership rates in the 1920s varied widely across counties and may have carried over into the 1930s. A number of states also changed their tax structures, spending on education, and rules about property. To account for this, the two research teams performed a regression analysis that estimates the effect of the HOLC on changes in housing markets while holding the other variables constant in a statistical sense. The regressions show that the relationship between the changes in home values and the HOLC loans per capita is still negative when the other factors are held constant. Counties with an additional dollar of HOLC loans per capita had an additional drop of $50.50 in median home values. After controlling for these factors in an analysis of the number of home owners, an additional dollar of HOLC loans per capita was associated with virtually no change in the number of nonfarm home owners.

**One More Step: Accounting for the HOLC's Attempts to Offset Housing Decline**

Thus far, it does not appear that the HOLC contributed to higher home values or to keeping people in their homes. But there is one more major issue that needs to be addressed. The HOLC program likely made more loans in hard-hit areas, where home values and the number of nonfarm owners were falling. Thus, the HOLC's focus on trying to stop declines in housing values and the number of home owners offsets the positive effects of the HOLC. In economics and statistics, this problem is known as negative endogeneity bias: the HOLC policies to help struggling housing markets counter any potential finding that the HOLC loans could have caused an increase in housing values and home ownership.

One method used to combat this problem is an instrumental variable analysis developed by econometricians, economists who specialize in applying statistical methods to economic data. The goal is to find features that influenced the HOLC's distribution of loans across the counties but did *not* directly influence housing values or home ownership after all of the other factors are included in the analysis. In essence, the goal is to find some feature of HOLC policy that strongly influenced housing markets *only through the HOLC loans* and not through an alternative avenue that has not been taken into account already in the analysis.

Both teams of researchers focused on the distance from HOLC offices as the key feature. The instrumental variable analysis then estimates a relationship between the HOLC loans per capita and the distance from HOLC offices as well as all of the other factors that influenced the HOLC. A predicted value for HOLC loans per capita for each county is calculated from this analysis. The predicted value captures the aspect of the HOLC that was related to distance from the offices but was not related to the HOLC's attempts to offset declines in housing values and in home ownership. The final step is to estimate the relationship between housing values and the predicted value of HOLC loans per capita. This step is also performed for the number of home owners. If the instrument operates only through the HOLC loans, the estimated relationships have been cleansed of the negative bias arising from the HOLC's attempts to correct the housing problems.

The research teams focused on the distance from HOLC offices because the HOLC loan process was more costly when the home was located in a city with no HOLC office. The application and loan process for the HOLC loans involved extensive paperwork, negotiations with the lender, evaluations of the value of the home, visits to the neighborhood to evaluate its impact on the value of the home, and a variety of other steps. The costs of all of these activities were substantially lower if the HOLC had an office in the same town as the home. As the distance between the home's county and the HOLC office's county rose, the processing costs also rose. Thus, we would expect fewer HOLC loans per capita in places that were farther from the HOLC offices.

There still remains a worry that the HOLC located offices in places where there were more mortgage problems, and thus the negative bias problem would not be fully resolved. Both research teams tried alternative methods and found similar results. One method involved creating an alternative distribution of offices for the HOLC based on a national administrator who was setting up offices to minimize the cost of reaching the most people without regard to the extent of housing problems. This alternative distribution called for the administrator to locate an office in each state capital to reduce the costs of interacting with state officials. In addition, the cost-focused administrator would locate an office in the four largest cities in each state to insure that it reached the largest number of home owners in the state. The HOLC actually established 244 offices in 228 counties. This alternative cost-based method called for offices in 204 counties. The research teams then calculated the distance from each county seat to the county seats in the 204 counties with the alternative HOLC offices and used those distances as the instrumental variable. There are 137 counties that had an HOLC office and would have had an artificial office; 91 counties had an actual HOLC office but would not have had an artificial office; and 67 counties had no HOLC office but would have had an artificial office.

The idea is the following: suppose there were two counties with very similar housing markets in 1930, but one was closer to an HOLC office than the other. This could happen quite easily; compare, for example, New York and New Jersey, which both had six offices in mid-1935. Since New York is a much larger state, many counties in New York did not have an HOLC office, even though they were of similar size to counties in New Jersey that did have offices. Essentially, this methodology systematically compares counties like those in New York with similar counties like those in New Jersey. The only difference arises because the New York counties are farther away from HOLC offices due to the idiosyncrasies of office location. Since the HOLC was presumably more active in areas near their offices, this allows the identification of the impact of the HOLC rather than confusing it with some other differences between counties.

The first step in the analysis showed that there was a strong negative relationship between HOLC loans per capita and the distance to the alternative offices, as expected. Thus, the alternative office scheme helped explain the distribution of HOLC loans per capita, but it was structured in such a way that the distance from the alternative offices would not be something that anybody would believe was related to problems in housing markets.

The results we discuss here are from a paper in the *Review of Financial Studies* in 2011 by the research team of Price Fishback, Alfonso Flores-Lagunes,

William Horrace, Shawn Kantor, and Jaret Treber. A paper in the *Journal of Economic History* by the research team of Charles Courtemanche and Kenneth Snowden in 2011 found similar results using different measures, HOLC activity and home-ownership rates, rather than the number of home owners.[1] After going through the instrumental variable process, the estimates suggest that a dollar increase in HOLC loans per capita in counties with less than fifty thousand people would have raised housing values by $115.70 in 1940. Similarly, an additional dollar would have raised the number of nonfarm home owners by 81.5 people (table A.1).

How much did the HOLC stave off the declines in housing? In the typical county with fewer than fifty thousand people, the median house value fell from $2,278 in 1930 to $1,431 in 1940. The mean of annual HOLC spending per capita was $1.90 in this sample. Based on the estimates above, when a county went from zero HOLC spending per capita to $1.90, the 1940 home value would have been $231.40 higher. Without the HOLC, the median house value would have fallen from $2,278 in 1930 to $1,200 in 1940. The $1,200

**Table A.1. Change in housing market variables associated with an additional dollar of HOLC loans per capita in counties with fewer than fifty thousand people as more controls are added to the analysis**

| | |
|---|---|
| House value in 1940 | $160.00 |
| Change in house value between 1930 and 1940 | −$75.00 |
| Change in house value 1930–1940 after controlling for changes in wide range of factors | −$50.50 |
| *Change in house value 1930–1940 after controlling for changes in wide range of factors and reducing negative bias* | $115.70 |
| | |
| Number of home owners in 1940 | 295 |
| Change in home owners between 1930 and 1940 | 45 |
| Change in home owners 1930–1940 after controlling for changes in wide range of factors | 6 |
| *Change in home owners 1930–1940 after controlling for changes in wide range of factors and reducing negative bias* | 81.5 |

figure comes from subtracting $231.40 from the mean of $1,431 for homes with a $1.90 of HOLC loans per capita. Therefore, the HOLC helped reduce a potential decline in housing values of 47 percent from $2,278 to $1,200 over the decade of the 1930s to a decline of only 37.2 percent from $2,278 to $1,431 (table A.2).

Remember that much of the decline in housing values occurred between 1930 and January 1934, which was about the time the HOLC began making loans. The Civil Works Administration survey implied an average drop of about 32 percent in home values during that time. If this was the average for all counties below fifty thousand people, the typical median value of housing would have fallen from $2,278 in 1930 to $1,549 by the beginning of 1934. Without the HOLC, the typical median house value would have fallen from $1,549 in 1934 to $1,200 in 1940, roughly a loss of $349 in value. Average HOLC loans per capita would have raised the price by $231.40 from $1,200 back to $1,431 in 1940. Thus, the HOLC loans per capita were able to stave off $231 or 69 percent of a potential decline of $349 in housing values between 1934 and 1940.

Comparisons of the 1930 and 1940 census for counties with fewer than fifty thousand people suggest that the average number of nonfarm home owners rose from 1,200 to 1,378 over the period. Without the HOLC average spending of $1.90 per capita, the typical county would have had only 1,223 home owners. The 1,223 figure is calculated as the average of 1,378 for counties in 1940, which would have experienced the average HOLC spending per capita of $1.90, minus $1.90 times the 81.5 increase in home owners associated with a dollar of HOLC spending per capita. Thus, with the HOLC the average number of nonfarm owners rose by 178 between 1930 and 1940, while without the HOLC it would have risen by only 23 over the decade. The HOLC therefore helped account for nearly all of the increase in the number of nonfarm home owners in a typical small county over the course of a decade.

We don't have good figures on the number of home owners in the mid-1930s. Comparisons of 1930 census home-ownership rates to home-ownership rates in a 1934 survey of 61 cities by the Civil Works Administration suggest an average drop in the home-ownership rate of about 3 percent. This seems roughly consistent with the rise in foreclosure rates to around 1 percent each year in the early 1930s. Thus, the number of home owners probably fell by about 3 percent between 1930 and the beginning of 1934. If the

**Table A.2. Evaluating the impact of HOLC spending per capita on nonfarm home values and the number of home owners in counties with fewer than fifty thousand people**

How much of the decline in median house value between 1930 and 1940 was prevented by HOLC?

| | | |
|---|---|---|
| A | Typical median house value in 1930 | $2,278 |
| B | Typical median house value in 1940, which incorporates the effect of an average HOLC loan per capita of $1.90 | $1,431 |
| C | Effect on typical median house value in 1940 of an added $1.90 of HOLC loans per capita ($1.90 times 115.70 effect of $1 of HOLC spending per capita) | $231 |
| D | Typical median house value in 1940 if county had received no HOLC loans (line B − line C) | $1,200 |
| E | Change in typical median house value between 1940 and 1930 with no HOLC loans (line A − line D) | $1,078 |
| F | HOLC loans prevented $231 loss out of $1,078 potential loss between 1930 and 1940 for a percentage of (line C ÷ line E) | 21.4% |

How much of the decline in median house value between 1934 and 1940 was prevented by HOLC?

| | | |
|---|---|---|
| G | Estimate of median house value in 1934 if it had allen by 32 percent between 1930 and 1934 (line A reduced by 32%) | $1,549 |
| H | Typical median house value in 1940, which incorporates the effect of an average HOLC loan per capita of $1.90 | $1,431 |
| I | Effect on typical median house value in 1940 of an added $1.90 of HOLC loans per capita ($1.90 times 115.70 effect of $1 of HOLC spending per capita) | $231 |
| J | Typical median house value in 1940 if county had received no HOLC loans (line H − line I) | $1,200 |
| K | Change in typical median house value between 1940 and 1934 with no HOLC loans (line G − line J) | $349 |
| L | HOLC loans prevented $231 loss out of $349 potential loss between 1934 and 1940 for a percentage of (line I ÷ line J) | 66.2% |

(*continued*)

**Table A.2** *(continued)*

How much of the increase in the number of home owners between 1930 and 1940 was contributed by the HOLC?

| | | |
|---|---|---:|
| M | Typical number of home owners in 1930 | 1,200 |
| N | Typical number of home owners in 1940, which incorporates the effect of an average HOLC loan per capita of $1.90 | 1,378 |
| O | Change in typical number of home owners between 1940 and 1930 (line N − line M) | 178 |
| P | Effect on typical number of home owners in 1940 of an added $1.90 of HOLC loans per capita ($1.90 times 81.5 increase in home owners associated with another dollar of HOLC spending per capita) | 155 |
| Q | HOLC loans helped account for 155 out of the 178 increase in home owners between 1930 and 1940 for a percentage of (line P ÷ line O) | 87.0% |

How much of the increase in the number of home owners between 1934 and 1940 was contributed by the HOLC?

| | | |
|---|---|---:|
| R | Estimate of number of home owners in 1934 if it had fallen by 3 percent between 1930 and 1934 (line M reduced by 3%) | 1,164 |
| S | Typical number of home owners in 1940, which incorporates the effect of an average HOLC loan per capita of $1.90 | 1,378 |
| T | Change in typical number of home owners between 1940 and 1934 (line S − line R) | 214 |
| U | Effect on typical number of home owners in 1940 of an added $1.90 of HOLC loans per capita ($1.90 times 81.5 increase in home owners associated with another dollar of HOLC spending per capita) | 155 |
| V | HOLC loans helped contribute 155 out of the 214 increase in home owners between 1934 and 1940 for a percentage of (line U ÷ line T) | 72.4% |

number of home owners fell 3 percent from the 1930 census average of 1,200, the typical number of home owners would have fallen from 1,200 to 1,164. Then, the typical number of home owners would have risen by 214 from 1,164 to 1,378 between 1934 and 1940. With $1.90 in HOLC spending per capita, the HOLC would have raised the number of home owners by 155, which is about 72 percent of the rise of 214 between 1934 and 1940 in a typical small county.

In chapter 9 we point out that neither research team could find a strong positive effect of the HOLC in counties with more than fifty thousand people. There are two potential reasons for this: either the HOLC had little impact there or the research teams could not effectively resolve the negative endogeneity bias. We discussed the reason that the HOLC might have had little impact in chapter 9. Here we discuss why the instrumental variable strategy designed to eliminate the negative bias may have been less effective for larger cities. The instrumental variable strategy worked for small towns because many of them were significant distances away from counties with HOLC offices. Many of the counties with more than fifty thousand people had HOLC offices. In fact, some like New York City, which was treated as one large area in both analyses, had several offices. Thus, the measured distance to an HOLC office or the artificial office was often zero for the larger cities. The instrument was therefore not as effective for large cities at picking out an aspect of HOLC lending that was not related to problems in housing markets. We are still working on this issue but have made little headway on it.

# Notes

PREFACE

1. Obama made his statement during the September 25, 2008, presidential debate. Clinton made her statement in "Let's Keep People in Their Homes," *Wall Street Journal*, September 25, 2008, accessed at http://online.wsj.com/article/SB122230767702474045 .html. McCain made his statement during the October 7, 2008, presidential debate. Shiller's statement is from an interview with Princeton University Press, accessed at http:// press.princeton.edu/releases/m8714.html. Blinder's statement is in "From the New Deal, a Way out of a Mess," *New York Times*, February 24, 2008, accessed at http://www .nytimes.com/2008/02/24/business/24view.html.

2. One strain of academic literature has discussed HOLC operations related to a practice that is known today as redlining. This literature is usually thought to begin with Jackson (1980), with notable contributions more recently including Hillier (2003) and Crossney and Bartelt (2005).

CHAPTER 1

1. See Home Owners' Loan Corporation Papers (hereafter HOLC Papers), Regional Correspondence Box 150. Joshua and Sarah Clark are pseudonyms for widower Joshua C. and his wife. Joshua's loan details were found in the HOLC records at the National Archives II in College Park, MD. We used a fictional last name to protect his privacy. In a turn of events that might have surprised him, Joshua's application files still exist, and may in fact be the only complete set of application files to the HOLC still extant. These files are part of a rare cache of documents that are buried in box 150 of the Regional Correspondence section of the HOLC. (Boxes 1 through 149 were, to be honest, less interesting.)

2. Unemployment statistics are discussed by Wallis (1989, 67).

3. Moratorium laws are discussed by Skilton (1943, 1944) and Wheelock (2008).

4. "1,000 Pray to Save Homes in Queens," *New York Times*, April 15, 1933, 15.

5. The phrase "through no fault of their own" is found in Federal Home Loan Bank Board (1938a, 28).

6. See HOLC Papers, Regional Correspondence Box 133 and Box 10.

CHAPTER 2

1. Although overall population growth slowed from 21 percent between 1900 and 1910 to 15 percent in the 1910s and 16 percent in the 1920s, there was a sharp rise in the nonfarm urban population and in the South and West. The share of population living in urban areas rose from 39.1 percent of the nonfarm population in 1900 to 45.1 percent in 1910, 51.2 percent in 1920, and 56.1 percent in 1930. The share of the urban population living in the South and West increased from 20.3 to 23.8, 25.9, and 29.1 percent over the same period.

2. The remarkable burst of home building during the 1920s figures prominently in several different explanations of the length and severity of the Great Depression. In the 1930s, scholars identified the 1920s as a peak in a recurrent series of fifteen- to eighteen-

year "long swings" in demographic-sensitive investment. Alvin Hansen (1964) later argued that the three "super-depressions" in the United States after the Civil War (those beginning in 1873, 1893, and 1929) all coincided with the beginning of a long-term downswing. Later investigations argued that the economy had produced an oversupply of housing by the late 1920s, which continued to depress the housing sector and the economy late into the 1930s; see Bolch, Fels, and McMahon (1971); Hickman (1960); and Gordon (1952). Most recently, Field (1992) argued that rigidities in the legal, regulatory, and financial environment appeared as urban boundaries were pushed outward in the 1920s—rigidities that inhibited recovery throughout the 1930s.

3. The volume of residential debt held by financial institutions and individual investors tripled from $9 to $30 billion between 1921 and 1929.

4. US Bureau of the Census (1923, table 23, pp. 130–33).

5. Grebler et al. (1956, 472–75) report that non-institutional investors held 42.5 percent of residential mortgage debt in 1920 and 37.5 percent of debt on one- to four-family homes in 1925.

6. H. Morton Bodfish (1931, 136) reports the figures for B&L growth, and Kenneth Snowden (2003, 169) describes the expansions in the South and West.

7. Lintner (1948, 412–14) performed the Massachusetts mutual savings bank study.

8. Morton (1956) describes the mix of lenders. The widespread use of short-term loans in midwestern mortgage markets before 1930 is also confirmed in a separate study of mortgage contracts written in 1928 in Chicago—eleven of these seventy loans were written for terms between two and four years while the remainder had terms of five years. See also Bodfish and Bayless (1928). Morton (1956, 150–52) reports that about one-half of a national sample of insurance company loans were written for terms of between five and nine years and another 20 percent for less than five years.

9. See Snowden (1997, 2003, 2010), and Snowden and James (2001) for more on B&L financing.

10. Bodfish and Bayless (1928); Bodfish (1935).

11. Gries and Ford (1932, 72–91) conducted the 1931 investigation.

12. See Alger (1934) and Chamberlain and Edwards (1927, 455), on the guarantee company activities.

13. The calculation of the real rate of interest is discussed in I. Fisher (1930, 526).

CHAPTER 3

1. Harriss (1951, 7–8).

2. The February 1938 *Federal Home Loan Bank Review* (190) estimated that 80 percent of foreclosures in metropolitan areas were on one- to four-family dwellings. This may have been a bit higher than for the nation as a whole, which includes nonmetropolitan areas. In the Cleveland metropolitan area from 1926 to 1933, 60 percent of foreclosures related to residential property, while the rest related primarily to stores and to vacant land. The rate was somewhat higher in the city itself, where there was less vacant land, as more of the development of vacant land had occurred in the suburbs than in the city itself during the 1920s. From 1926 to 1933, it appears that 17 percent of residential mortgages ended in foreclosure in Cleveland: the 1930 census indicates there were 81,155 owned homes in Cleveland in 1930, and conservatively assuming that 70 percent were mortgaged (as

was the case in 1934 according to Green 1935), the 9,646 foreclosures reported by Green (1934) indicate a 17 percent overall foreclosure rate.

3. See the February 2010 *Monetary Policy Report* for a discussion of foreclosure start data, http://www.federalreserve.gov/monetarypolicy/mpr_20100224_part2.htm, as well as the "Calculated Risk" blog, http://www.calculatedriskblog.com/2012/05/lps -march-foreclosure-starts-increase.html.

4. See Wickens (1937). Metro areas with the highest rates of borrowers who were more than ninety days delinquent on their mortgages experienced peaks in this serious delinquency in 2009. Las Vegas and Miami peaked at just around 25 percent of homes in serious delinquency. See Urban Institute (2010).

5. See Skilton (1944) for a list of states with mortgage moratoria.

6. National home-ownership rates are from US Bureau of the Census (2011, table 14).

7. Foote, Gerardi, and Willen (2008) develop a model showing the double trigger.

8. The estimates for 1929 and 1933 are from Carter et al. (2006), from the following series: nominal hourly and weekly earnings in manufacturing, Ba4381 and Ba4382; total employment on non-agricultural payrolls, Ba840 2–112; civilian private nonfarm labor force, Ba475 2–82; and manufacturing average weekly hours, Cb49 3–123. The wage figures were adjusted for inflation by national consumer price index with 1967 = 100 (series E135), and the unemployment rate (series D86) comes from Stanley Lebergott's estimates that include work-relief workers among the unemployed from US Bureau of the Census (1975, 135, 210–11).

9. The information on incomes is from table C4 in Wickens (1941, 183), adjusted by the national consumer price index with 1967 = 100 from US Bureau of the Census (1975, 210–11).

10. The most commonly used national housing price index available for the period between World War I and World War II shows that house prices reached a peak in 1925. The series then shows prices declining mildly until 1929, followed by a steep decline with a trough in 1933, about 30 percent below peak. This part of the series was constructed from the 1934 survey of over fifty cities of home owners used in figure 3.2. The home owners were asked to estimate the market value of their homes in 1934 as well as in the year they bought the homes. The data appear as series Dc826–828 in Carter et al. (2006). Unlike modern housing price indexes built on actual market prices, the price series is only as accurate as home owners' ability to estimate their property's market price in 1934 and to remember its market value years earlier.

11. The Federal Reserve Board's March 2011 *Monetary Policy Report* gives three price indexes, from CoreLogic, S&P/Case-Shiller, and the Federal Housing Finance Administration.

12. Annual lending estimates come from the Federal Home Loan Bank Board, published in Carter et al. (2006, series Dc983–989).

13. See I. Fisher (1933) and Mishkin (1978).

14. Life insurance company information is from series X-894–X-907 in US Bureau of the Census (1975, 1058–59). Commercial bank information is from series X-585 on page 1019. The decline in total assets/liabilities in series X-581 was similar. The B&L information is from Cj389 and Cj395 of Carter et al. (2006).

CHAPTER 4

1. US House of Representatives, *Congressional Record*, April 27, 1933, 2482, 2476.

2. See Skilton (1944) for a list of states with mortgage moratoria.

3. Alston (1984) and Wheelock (2008) investigate the determinants of adoption of mortgage moratoria across states.

4. See Harvard Law Review (1934). This unsigned article notes that the Supreme Court in its Blaisdell decision "brought the trend of precedent sharply to a halt" by deciding "that laws altering existing contracts constitute an impairment within the meaning of the contract clause only if they are unreasonable in the light of the circumstances occasioning their enactment."

5. The moratoria also had longer-run unintended impacts on the supply of credit, as discussed in Bridewell (1938) and Alston (1984).

6. See Ewalt (1962, chap. 4).

7. For the Cochran quote, see US House of Representatives, *Congressional Record*, April 25, 1933, 2345.

8. "The President's Message," *New York Times*, April 14, 1933, 2.

9. For descriptions of these legislative developments, see "Will Ask Changes in Home Loan Bill," *New York Times*, April 20, 1933, 8; "Bar $20,000 Limit in Mortgage Bill," *New York Times*, April 28, 1933, 14; "Mortgage Bill Passes House," *New York Times*, April 29, 1933, 4. The 1930 shares of owned homes come from US Bureau of the Census (1933, 17).

10. Federal Home Loan Bank Board (1937, 28).

11. For descriptions of declines in income throughout the income distribution between 1929 and 1933, see Menderhausen (1946).

12. The prayer meetings in New York were described in "1,000 Pray to Save Homes in Queens," *New York Times*, April 15, 1933, 15. Fleck (1999) and Fishback, Kantor, and Wallis (2003) show that voter turnout strongly influenced the distribution of New Deal funds to counties during the New Deal.

13. Jones's introduction of the bill is described in "Senate to Hasten Bankruptcy Aid," *New York Times*, February 19, 1933, 6.

14. See Johnson (1973) for a description of the timing and structure of the farm mortgage crisis of the 1920s.

15. Engberg (1931, 133).

16. Olsen (1933) details the farm foreclosure data. Schwartz (1938, chaps. 10, 11) documents the failure of the joint-stock land banks and the role of the Emergency Farm Mortgage Act of 1933 in their liquidation.

17. For contemporary accounts of the condition of the farm mortgage market in early 1933, see "Iowa Governor Asks Halt on Foreclosure," *New York Times*, January 20, 1933, 2; "See No Moratoria Cure" and "Gov. Horner Asks Mortgage Mercy," *New York Times*, February 5, 1933, 2.

18. The similarity and differences between the farm and urban mortgage situations are discussed in "Farm Mortgages: A Pressing National Issue," *New York Times*, February 5, 1933, sec. 8.

19. "Realty Bill Seeks Immediate Relief," *New York Times*, March 19, 1933, RE1. It was significant that Roosevelt could presume that parallel approaches to the farm and home mortgage crises were politically acceptable, because the two cases differed in at least

two important respects. First, foreclosure meant a loss not only of a residence but also a livelihood for farmers. Second, the federal government was much more deeply involved in the farm mortgage market through the Federal Farm Loan Bank system than in the residential market, given the slow start of the FHLB. The performance of the FHLB was so disappointing by 1933, in fact, that drafts of the HOLC bill called for its elimination. Despite these differences, statements both in Congress and by many governors combined the farm and home foreclosure crises and characterized both as deserving support. An explanation could be that foreclosures involved similar legal and procedural issues that did not depend on the nature of the property.

20. Prominent New York real estate professionals and attorneys spoke in support of action to shut off the crisis. See "Interest Rate Cuts Aid Realty Market" and "Second Mortgage Fund Is Urged for the Relief of Home Owners," *New York Times*, January 20, 1933, RE1; "Suspension of Mortgage Amortization Proposed" and "Mortgage Rates Present Problem," *New York Times*, February 5, 1933, RE1; and "Realty Interest Centres in Tax and Mortgage Rates," February 12, 1933, 150–51. Action was also called for by the American Construction Council, of which president-elect Roosevelt was the honorary president; see "Protective Steps for Realty Owner," *New York Times*, February 12, 1933, 38. Action was also called for by the statewide Real Estate Board of New York and its individual local affiliates; see "Realty Bill Seeks Immediate Relief," *New York Times*, March 19, 1933, RE1.

21. The quote, which captures the sentiment of many in the housing field on many bills, came from a member of the mortgage committee of the National Association of Real Estate Boards when supporting a bill before the New York legislature in March 1933; see "Realty Bill Seeks Immediate Relief," *New York Times*, March 19, 1933, RE1.

22. See interview with Charles G. Moses, a "well-known New York Realty man," in *New York Times*, January 20, 1933, RE1. A reading of the *New York Times* between January and March 1933 reveals proposals to reduce mortgage rates and property taxes and a variety of calls for stays on foreclosure by lenders and local tax authorities (January 4, 35; January 20, 2, 20; January 24, 13; February 5, 2, RE1, N7; February 12, 15, 38; February 14, 36; February 17, 5; February 19, 6; March 19, RE1). For other calls for voluntary action rather than legislation, see *New York Times*, February 5, 2, RE1. A survey of New York loans in the 1920s and 1930s (not including HOLC loans) shows no signs of principal reductions in any of the mortgage modifications; see Ghent (2011).

23. For example, the problem with tax sales became so severe in New Jersey by February 1933 that specific legislation was introduced in the state legislature to eliminate interest charges on delinquent property taxes and to suspend property tax land sales; see "Hague Maps Bill to Bar Tax Sales," *New York Times*, February 17, 1933, 5.

24. Beito (1989, 11–15) documents the activities of the NAREB's Property Owners Division across the nation in calling for lower tax rates and local government spending. He acknowledges the HOLC's important role in effectively ending the public property tax discussion late in 1933.

25. See Harriss (1951, 11).

CHAPTER 5
1. *Foreclosure* refers to the act of eliminating the borrower's right to own and control the encumbered property. When this right has been foreclosed, the property can be sold

or seized by the lender or a third party (in deed-of-trust states) for the purpose of satisfying claims under the loan contract.

2. The New York study is by Nicholas and Scherbina (2012). A modern study by Pennington-Cross (2006) shows that foreclosed properties tend to sell for a price about 22–24 percent lower than similar property that has not gone through foreclosure. See Ghent (2011) for discussions about delays between foreclosure proceedings and the sale of the home.

3. Among loan modifications, 7 percent experienced interest rate increases, 6.5 percent called for an increase in the principal owed, and 17 percent called for a partial prepayment (Ghent 2011, table 2). Data on the shares of loans modified and foreclosed are drawn from table 2 and figure 1 in Ghent (2011). This sample for New York is part of a larger sample of mortgages designed to cover loans originating between 1920 and 1934. See Morton (1956) for a detailed description of the sample and its potential biases. Note that for all of the New York loans studied that originated between 1920 and the early 1940s, the probability that a loan would have been foreclosed on was 16.5 percent, the probability it would have been modified was 47 percent, and the probability that it received a second modification was 22.1 percent (Ghent 2011, table 1). Once the HOLC was in place purchasing and modifying large numbers of loans in 1934, lenders more actively pursued foreclosure at the expense of modification, as the foreclosure rate rose to 3 percent and the modification rate fell to 5 percent of the loans. The situation even worsened in 1935, as the foreclosure rate among the New York sample loans peaked at 7 percent and the loan modification rate rose to 9 percent (Ghent 2011, table 2).

4. The national number of foreclosures is from figure 3.1. The New York sample ratio rose from 0.1 in 1932 to 0.18 in 1933, 0.63 in 1934, and 0.78 in 1935.

5. For an overview of these multiple-lender issues in the 1920s and 1930s, see Snowden (1995, 2010). The Schackno Act allowed the New York Insurance Commissioner to modify mortgages with the agreement of two-thirds of investors, removing the need for unanimous consent. Reep (1928, chap. 11) describes the problems that arose with second mortgages. For discussion about the modern problems with securitization, see Piskorski, Seru, and Vig (2010), who find that securitized loans were more likely to foreclose than similar bank-held loans. They infer that this could reflect different rates of modification. See also a skeptical discussion of these results by Adelino, Gerardi, and Willen (2010). In contrast, Foote, Gerardi, Goette, and Willen (2009) and Adelino, Gerardi, and Willen (2009) note that modification may not be in the interest of lenders if they cannot target the loans that would benefit from modification (either because of asymmetric information or because of moral hazard) or if there is a meaningful probability of redefault after the modification. The lack of such information may be a more subtle but important impediment.

6. The study of foreclosure costs was conducted by the HOLC and is described in *Federal Home Loan Bank Review*, November 1937, 40–45.

7. "Legislation Is Sought to Curb Foreclosures," *New York Times*, April 9, 1933, RE2.

8. Bernanke, Gertler, and Gilchrist (1996) conceptualized the financial accelerator. Courtemanche and Snowden (2011) describe the mortgage market from this perspective.

9. This is precisely the thinking behind the current Home Affordable Modification

Program (HAMP), in which public subsidies are used to encourage servicers and lenders to provide modifications.

10. Though there are assertions of strategic defaults during the 1930s, there is no hard evidence. In the modern era, Mayer et al. (2011) used a natural experiment at Countrywide to uncover evidence of strategic defaults. Countrywide borrowers in different states faced different incentives to default as some but not all state governments brought lawsuits against Countrywide, which ultimately agreed to offer modifications to borrowers in default.

11. See Harriss (1951, 12–14), about the application dates. More details about HOLC legislation and administration are in chapter 6.

12. The publication of rejection statistics is seen in *New York Times*, October 14, 1933, 28, and October 29, 1933, N7.

13. C. Lowell Harriss discusses the mechanics of the HOLC's bond issuance more in his 1951 book.

14. The effect of interest rate guarantees is discussed in more depth in chapter 8.

15. To make this calculation, we set up a fifteen-year amortized repayment schedule for a $1,000 loan at 6 percent interest. Investment A involved one hundred loans that were fully repaid on schedule. Using a 6 percent discount rate, each loan had a present value of $1,000, so the present value of investment A was $100,000. Investment B in one hundred loans mimicked the HOLC experience. Eighty percent of the $1,000 loans were fully repaid along the standard repayment schedule, and 20 percent of the loans made no payments for three years, at which time there were foreclosures and the properties were sold for 70 percent of their value. The present value at a 6 percent discount rate of each fully repaid loan was $1,000, while the present value for each foreclosed loan was $565.84. The expected present value for investment B is $917,555 ($= 80 \times 1000 + 20 \times 565.84$). The internal rate of return for investment B that leads to a present value equal to the $100,000 present value for investment A is 7.35 percent. The 1.35 percent difference between 6 percent on risk-free investment and 7.35 percent on the risky investment is the "risk premium" that a investor who does not care about risk would demand on investment B so that the expected present value of the two investments is the same. The risk premium varies at different interest rates. When starting with risk-free loan rates and discount rates of 5 percent interest rate, the risk premium was slightly lower at 1.25 percent. With risk-free loan and discount rates of 3 percent interest, the risk premium was 1.08 percent.

CHAPTER 6

1. See Harriss (1951, 33). His proportion of one-fifth is based on a rough estimate of the total number of homes under mortgage in the early 1930s. More precise estimates would have been available to Harriss (and to us) if the question about mortgage encumbrance had not been omitted from the 1930 census.

2. Nonfarm home ownership was lower in the 1930s than today, while residential mortgage debt was a much smaller share of GDP. The $3 billion in HOLC loans in 1933 compares with $56.4 billion in nominal GDP in 1933, or 5.3 percent (5.3 percent of 2012 GDP of around $15.5 trillion is around $820 billion). But home ownership has risen from around 45 percent in 1930 to a peak around 69 percent in 2007, the value of homes has risen, and the share of the value mortgaged has risen.

3. For example, this contrasts with the Federal Farm Mortgage Corporation, which was set up as part of an analogous relief effort for farm mortgage borrowers. Its lending authority was originally designed to expire in 1936 like the HOLC but was repeatedly extended up to 1947.

4. Technically, this means the HOLC was a mortgage refinance program. We have called it a mortgage modification program in the past, as it can be thought of as modifying the way borrowers paid their debts in an effort to avoid foreclosure.

5. See HOLC (1933). The structure of the HOLC contrasts with contemporary mortgage modification programs enacted by the federal government in the wake of the recent housing market distress. These programs have not attempted to bring distressed mortgages held by private lenders under government control. Rather, they have opted for a structure in which they encourage lenders to implement modifications by themselves. Given this structure, different approaches had to been taken to provide relief for lenders holding troubled assets, mainly through capital investments by the government in lenders.

6. Shares of homes not eligible for HOLC loans are based on 1930 figures for families from US Bureau of the Census (1933, 17 and 60).

7. The Stevenson quote and discussion of early requirements are from Stevenson (1933, 1). Even in the first report and in Stevenson's initial discussions of the HOLC, HOLC officials constantly talk about the program as being for mortgages already in distress. See Federal Home Loan Bank Board (1934, 4, 48–50). Their later amendments and discussions in reports imply that they meant people in distress through no fault of their own. The April 27 amendment and quote are from Federal Home Loan Bank Board (1936, 27, 53). See also the 1936 annual report of the Federal Home Loan Bank Board (1937, 29).

8. The benefits to lenders and borrowers are discussed in depth in chapters 7 and 8.

9. See Courtemanche and Snowden (2011, table 1).

10. More than three thousand B&Ls had failed by 1933 along with nearly the entire mortgage guarantee industry that served individual investors. Both types of institutions then entered protracted liquidations. See Snowden (2010).

11. Rose (2012) discusses how B&Ls created bad banks in the 1930s during reorganization proceedings. In recent memory, well-known bad banks have included the Resolution Trust Corporation, which collected the assets of failed savings and loan associations during the late 1980s and 1990s, and bad banks set up in Sweden and Finland during banking crises in those countries. See Hawkins and Turner (1999) for a comparative review of bad banks in several countries during the 1980s and 1990s. Modern readers may be surprised to find that bad banks were used widely during the 1930s as a resolution technique by a variety of financial firms.

12. See Stevenson (1933, 1–2), for a discussion.

13. The debate over the HOLC guarantee was also motivated by the fact that the federal government already guaranteed bonds issued by the Federal Farm Mortgage Corporation in its farm mortgage debt refinancing operations. Roosevelt used this language in a March 1, 1934, message to Congress. "Message to Congress Recommending Legislation to Guarantee Principal on Home Owners Loan Bonds," available online from Ger-

hard Peters and John T. Woolley, *The American Presidency Project*, http://www.presidency
.ucsb.edu/ws/?pid=14816.

14. US House of Representatives (1934, 42, 84).

15. See Harriss (1951, 25–29).

16. "Home Owners' Loan Corporation Opens First Office in New York," *New York Times*, August 15, 1933, 19.

17. The development of the HOLC is described in Federal Home Loan Bank Board (1934, 47–69; 1935, 81–89; and 1936, 52–79).

18. See the Testimony of Horace A. Russell in US Senate, Subcommittee of the Committee on Banking and Currency (1933, 10).

19. Information on loans and staffing comes from Federal Home Loan Bank Board (1941, 160) and Federal Home Loan Bank Administration (1952, 10).

CHAPTER 7

1. The discussion of Prudential's attitude is found in HOLC Papers, General Loan Correspondence Box 133: Memo from S. J. Christie, Michigan State Manager, to Mr. Paul J. Frissell, National Office Assistant General Manager, August 6, 1935, "Re: Ingham #998-A, Harry M. C., Lansing, Michigan."

2. The chairman of the HOLC described this situation in a Senate hearing in 1934. See US House of Representatives (1934, 13).

3. HOLC Papers, Regional Office Correspondence Box 133: Letter from Wade Van Valkenberg to R. W. McCutcheson, February 18, 1935, "Re: J. Julia C."

4. HOLC Papers, Regional Office Correspondence Box 133: Letter from Wade Van Valkenberg to R. W. McCutcheson, February 18, 1935, "Re: J. Julia C."

5. "First Home Loan Aids Needy Owner," *New York Times*, August 31, 1933, 19.

6. See *Federal Home Loan Bank Review*, July 1941, 336; and Harriss (1951, 25).

7. Skilton (1944) points out that the HOLC did not use this appraisal strategy when acquiring loans through foreclosure, instead relying on estimates of current market value. This underscores that HOLC officials deliberately chose not to base appraisals on current market value for underwriting purposes.

8. The sample of loans was made available to C. Lowell Harriss of the National Bureau of Economic Research. Harriss (1951, 32–33) presented information on the average HOLC loan-to-appraisal ratio for each state as a whole but never looked at the underlying market prices. The data were microfilmed and sat in a box at the offices of the National Bureau of Economic Research in New York for more than fifty years. In 2008 Jonathan Rose inquired about the survival of the records. By pure coincidence the microfilm had been catalogued only the week before. Jonathan digitized the data, which are now available from the NBER's website. http://www.nber.org/nberhistory/historical archives/archives.html.

9. The appraisal process is reviewed in detail by Rose (2011). The HOLC appraisal was the result of averaging three figures: an estimate of market price, an estimate of rental income, and an estimate of the cost of buying a similar property and building similar improvements. Rose describes how the market prices tended to be the lowest of the three estimates, leading to appraisals that on average exceeded the market price. As noted, this was a deliberate decision by HOLC officials, as they did not view the current

market price as necessarily reflecting the value of the property as collateral, and because of the importance of high appraisals for negotiating with lenders. The appraisal also had a discretionary component, as the three-part average was reviewed by a committee, and these discretionary movements tended to be accommodative particularly in those cases where higher appraisals mattered for the 80 percent limit.

10. HOLC Papers, General Administrative Correspondence Roll 21: Memo from Dalton G. De Witt to Philip Kniskern, March 27, 1934, "Re: Appraisal Situation in New Jersey." The reference to "bailing out the owner" in the quote is somewhat ironic, since higher appraisals made it more difficult for the HOLC to reduce the amount of the debt that the home owner owed when the loan was refinanced. The best interpretation is likely that HOLC officials believed admission to the program was a significant benefit in itself, regardless of whether some of the borrower's debt was reduced.

11. HOLC Papers, General Administrative Correspondence Roll 13: Memo from Patrick Kennedy, State Manager of Connecticut, to Horace Russell, October 27, 1933.

12. See Federal Home Loan Bank Board (1938b, 70).

13. This approval of second mortgages was not acknowledged in any official HOLC literature, but Harriss (1951, 35–37) mentions it, as did an HOLC official in testimony before Congress in 1934. See US House of Representatives (1934, 55–57).

14. At first, the HOLC issued bonds with 4 percent interest rates. These bonds were guaranteed only as to their principal payments. After the HOLC was given the authority to issue bonds fully guaranteed as to both interest and principal, it issued bonds with 3 percent interest rates. Those lenders who had received the earlier 4 percent issues were given the option of replacing those bonds with the new, fully guaranteed bonds at the lower 3 percent interest rate. Skilton (1944) discusses this a bit further.

CHAPTER 8

1. HOLC Papers, Regional Office Correspondence Box 133: Letter from Anna J. C. to Mrs. Franklin D. Roosevelt, October 28, 1935.

2. US Senate, Subcommittee of the Committee on Banking and Currency (1933, 28).

3. HOLC Papers, Regional Office Correspondence Box 133: Letter from Lee E. Kuhlman to Harold Lee, April 9, 1934, "Re: Lee C."

4. HOLC Papers, Regional Office Correspondence Box 133: Letter from Carroll F. Sweet to John B. Dew, December 19, 1935, "Re: Raymond C."

5. For example, suppose an $1,800 mortgage loan had been taken out on a home with a value that had dropped from $3,000 to $2,000. It would require a $600 payment to reestablish a 60 percent loan-to-value ratio.

6. The original act provided that the borrower need not pay any principal on his indebtedness for three years after June 13, 1933. This provision was stricken from the act by the amendment of April 27, 1934; see Federal Home Loan Bank Board (1935, 31).

7. The unemployment rate used here treats relief workers as unemployed and was estimated by Stanley Lebergott and reported in chapter D in US Bureau of the Census (1975). Michael Darby (1976) reported lower rates of 21 percent in 1933 and 9 percent in 1937 when treating relief workers as employed. In making comparisons of unemployment with the modern era, a case can be made that relief workers in the 1930s should

be treated as unemployed. The relief worker's hourly wage was about half the wage on federal public works projects at the time, and the number of hours he or she could work was restricted. Thus, the share of wages paid to relief workers is similar to the share of wages paid to people on unemployment insurance today. The difference is that the relief workers had to do work to get their unemployment checks.

8. Wickens (1941, 254).

9. Average annual income of $1,155 and the 8 percent interest rate is reported in Wickens (1937, xxvi, xxviii). We have calculated the monthly payments by determining an annuity for the annual payment for a principal of $2,272 and then dividing the annual payment by twelve.

10. Federal Home Loan Bank Board (1941, 143).

11. See Federal Home Loan Bank Board (1941, 140); and Federal Home Loan Bank Administration (1947, 32). By the end of fiscal year 1945, nearly 50 percent of the loan accounts had been terminated, 20 percent through foreclosure and 30 percent through prepayment.

12. See Federal Home Loan Bank Board (1941, 143, 145–48) and Federal Home Loan Bank Administration (1947, 33).

13. The Boise average home price comes from Wickens (1941, 97).

14. The market prices were not necessarily accurate in every case, but as long as they were not systematically biased in one direction, these aggregate figures are meaningful.

15. The 7 percent figure comes from Federal Home Loan Bank Board (1938b, 70). The NBER sample indicates that most of this debt was likely forgiven by second-lien holders. It is not clear, though, whether this takes into account the new second liens that the HOLC allowed some second mortgage holders to create as compensation for losing their previous claims.

16. Of the 198,215 properties acquired by the HOLC, 170,237 (86 percent) were acquired by the end of 1939 (Harriss 1951, 191).

17. See Skilton (1944, 179).

18. The HOLC Act specified 5 percent as the maximum rate for HOLC loans. As a result, the board needed no additional authority to lower the rate in 1939.

19. See Federal Home Loan Bank Board (1940, 1941).

20. Harriss (1951) and Federal Home Loan Bank Board (1941, 142) describe the ways in which HOLC officials acted as social workers to help troubled borrowers.

21. See Federal Home Loan Bank Board (1940, 28).

22. Foreclosure forbearance through 1937 is described in Federal Home Loan Bank Board (1937, 28). Forbearance through 1941 comes from Federal Home Loan Bank Board (1941, 150).

23. HOLC Papers, Regional Office Correspondence Box 151: Mortgagor Case Analysis Report, April 1936, "Re: Frank and Ellen W."

24. HOLC Papers, Regional Office Correspondence Box 50: Summary and Recommendation, July 23, 1936, "Re: Katherin C."

25. Abrams (1946, 245).

26. HOLC Papers, Regional Office Correspondence Box 8: Summary and Recommendation, July 1, 1936, "Re: Antonio and Nancy C."

27. HOLC Papers, Regional Office Correspondence Box 50: Delinquent Loan Report, September 17, 1935, "Re: Miriam E. C."

28. HOLC Papers, Regional Office Correspondence Box 8: Report on Property Proposed for Foreclosure or Voluntary Deed, February 13, 1936, "Re: Edwin and Nancy C."

29. Rose and Snowden (2012) examine the history of the modern loan contract and why it was adopted widely during the 1930s.

CHAPTER 9

1. Federal Home Loan Bank Board (1936, 60).

2. Average home-price drop is from Wickens (1941, table A10).

3. Prices by city are from Wickens (1941, table A10).

4. This section on the distribution of HOLC activity across counties is based on Courtemanche and Snowden (2011). See also Fishback, Kantor, and Wallis (2003) for county-level studies of the HOLC and a number of other New Deal programs. For studies of distributions of funds from New Deal programs, see Fishback, Kantor, and Wallis (2003); Fleck (2008); Wallis (1998); Reading (1973); Wright (1974); and the papers cited in those studies.

5. Recall that the HOLC program was focused on nonfarm homes. As we discussed in chapter 4, there was an alternative program for farm owners through the Farm Credit Administration. Throughout the rest of the chapter, therefore, we need to emphasize that we are referring only to nonfarm owners and nonfarm housing values unless otherwise noted.

6. See Courtemanche and Snowden (2011) and Fishback et al. (2011).

7. The results we discuss here are from Fishback et al. (2011). Courtemanche and Snowden (2011) report similar results while using different measures of HOLC activity and home-ownership rates rather than the number of home owners.

8. In order to successfully use the "distance from office" approach, Fishback et al. (2011) exclude the 395 counties from their sample that had populations above fifty thousand in 1930; as a result, their estimated impacts for the HOLC program apply only to counties with lower populations. Courtemanche and Snowden (2011) use the "distance from office" approach by removing from the sample the 209 counties in which an HOLC office was located in the spring of 1934. See below for a discussion of the differences in the interpretation of HOLC impacts in these excluded markets.

9. Fishback et al. (2011) found some evidence that counties where the HOLC loaned more per capita experienced a larger increase in the number of renters. Given that the HOLC's support of home owners would have reduced the supply of rental housing, the only way this could have occurred is if lenders had made a significant number of loans for new apartment construction. The finding is puzzling because neither set of researchers could find any evidence that the HOLC loans were associated with increases in building activity.

CHAPTER 10

1. The *Time* magazine article was downloaded from http://www.time.com/time/magazine/article/0,9171,792832,00.html on October 14, 2011. See also Tough (1951) for an early examination of the profitability of the HOLC.

2. See also Mason (2004, 113) and Winston (1979).

3. The HOLC final report gave a final net earnings figure of $14,068,588.64, of which $13,993,588.64 was paid into the US Treasury. See Home Loan Bank Board (1952, vi). In an audit of the Federal Home Loan Bank Board, which included the HOLC, the Comptroller General of the United States (1953, 9) reported that the net earnings of the HOLC from its inception to June 30, 1952, was $13,993,589.

4. According to the Bureau of Labor Statistics Consumer Price Index calculator at the www.bls.gov website.

5. See the report by the Comptroller General of the United States (1953, 9, 27–28).

6. Comparisons are based on bond rates listed in schedule 4 in Home Loan Bank Board 1952 and yields on high-grade corporate bonds reported in series Cj1238 through Cj1242 in James and Sylla (2006, 3–826).

7. Busby is quoted in US House of Representatives (1934, 84).

8. Roosevelt's statement is from "Message to Congress Recommending Legislation to Guarantee Principal on Home Owners Loan Bonds," March 1, 1934. Online at Gerhard Peters and John T. Woolley, The American Presidency Project, http://www.presidency.ucsb.edu/ws/?pid=14816.

9. Comparisons based on bond rates listed in Home Loan Bank Board (1952, schedule 4), and yields on high-grade corporate bonds reported in James and Sylla (2006, series Cj1238–Cj1242).

10. Abrams (1946, 246).

CHAPTER 11

1. In particular, the legislative history of H4H makes clear that the HOLC was studied as a precedent and that the HOLC bad bank model was explicitly set aside due to concerns over purchasing loans out of securitization pools. Some of H4H's proponents even predicted the H4H would be "a modern equivalent of the HOLC," though a careful study of the HOLC indicates several important differences. See, for example, the testimony of Ellen Harnick, senior policy counsel of the Center for Responsible Lending (US Senate Committee on Banking, Housing, and Urban Affairs 2008).

2. The original maximum loan-to-value ratio in H4H was 90 percent. This was increased to 96.5 percent in November 2008 for borrowers with relatively high credit scores. The program also had an important requirement that if borrowers sold their homes in the future, they share the gains from any price appreciation with the federal government.

3. Some payments are one-time, and other payments recur over time depending on the status of the loan. All HAMP loans are designed to have a positive return to lenders. The program proceeds with a modification only if the lender agrees and if the revenue post-modification (including payments from the Treasury and payments from borrowers post-modification) exceed the expected revenue from loans without modification.

4. Brian Collins, "No One at All Happy with Modification Results," Mortgage Servicing News, September 1, 2011.

5. HAMP figures are from Home Affordable Program (2012, 1–6). Number of home owners in 2010 was about 76 million, from http://factfinder2.census.gov/faces/tableservices/jsf/pages/productview.xhtml?pid=DEC_10_DP_DPDP1&prodType=table, downloaded on August 23, 2012.

6. Lenders and servicers were always encouraged to grant principal reductions vol-

untarily through HAMP, but in practice few HAMP modifications involved such actions. In October 2010, the Obama administration initiated a program to encourage voluntary principal reductions, but it has only modified about 60,000 loans, compared to 1.1 million for HAMP permanent modification as of April 2012. For figures see Making Home Affordable Program (2012, 1–6).

7. See Raskin (2011) and Cordell et al. (2008).

8. Discussion of the Fannie and Freddie investments can be found in Pro Publica (2012).

9. Nominal GDP averaged $69.9 billion between 1933 and 1936 when the HOLC purchased $3 billion of loans (Carter et al. 2006, series Ca74).

APPENDIX

1. See Fishback et. al. (2011) and Courtemanche and Snowden (2011).

# References

Abrams, Charles. 1946. *The Future of Housing*. New York: Harper and Brothers.

Adelino, Manuel, Kristopher Gerardi, and Paul Willen. 2009. "Why Don't Lenders Renegotiate More Home Mortgages? Redefaults, Self-Cures and Securitization." National Bureau of Economic Research Working Paper 15159.

———. 2010. "What Explains Differences in Foreclosure Rates? A Response to Piskorski, Seru, and Vig." Atlanta Federal Reserve Working Paper 2010–8.

Alger, George. 1934. *Report on the Operation, Conduct, and Management of Title and Mortgage Guarantee Corporations*. Moreland Commission Report No. 38. Albany, NY.

Alston, Lee. 1984. "Farm Foreclosure Moratorium Legislation: A Lesson from the Past." *American Economic Review* 74, no. 3: 445–57.

Beito, David. 1989. *Taxpayers in Revolt: Tax Resistance during the Great Depression*. Chapel Hill: University of North Carolina Press.

Bernanke, Ben, Mark Gertler, and Simon Gilchrist. 1996. "The Financial Accelerator and the Flight to Quality." *Review of Economics and Statistics* 78, no. 1: 1–15.

Bodfish, Morton. 1931. *History of Building and Loan in the United States*. New York: Prentice Hall.

———. 1935. *The Depression Experience of Savings and Loan Associations in the United States*. Chicago: United States Building and Loan League.

Bodfish, Morton, and A. C. Bayless. 1928. "Costs and Encumbrance Ratios in a Highly Developed Real Estate Market." *Journal of Land & Public Utility Economics* 4, no. 2: 125–38.

Bolch, B., R. Fels, and M. McMahon. 1971. "Housing Surplus in the 1920s?" *Explorations in Economic History* 8, no. 3: 259–83.

Bridewell, David A. 1938. "The Effects of Defective Mortgage Laws on Home Financing." *Law and Contemporary Problems* 5, no. 4: 545–63.

Carter, Susan B., Scott S. Gartner, Michael R. Haines, Alan L. Olmstead, Richard Sutch, and Gavin Wright, eds. 2006. *Historical Statistics of the United States, Earliest Times to the Present*. Millennial edition. New York: Cambridge University Press.

Chamberlain, Lawrence, and George W. Edwards. 1927. *The Principles of Bond Investment*. New York: Henry Holt and Company.

Comptroller General of the United States. 1953. *Report on Audit of the Financial Statements and Accounts of the Home Loan Bank Board and the Organizations under Its Supervision for the Year Ended June 30, 1952*. H.R. Document No. 52, 83rd Congress, 1st session. Washington, DC: Government Printing Office.

Cordell, Larry, Karen Dynan, Andreas Lehnert, Nellie Liang, and Eileen Mauskopf. 2008. "The Incentive of Mortgage Servicers." Federal Reserve Board FEDS Working Paper 2008–46.

Courtemanche, Charles, and Kenneth Snowden. 2011. "Repairing a Mortgage Crisis: HOLC Lending and Its Impact on Local Housing Markets." *Journal of Economic History* 71, no. 2: 307–37.

Crossney, Kristen B., and David W. Bartelt. 2005. "The Legacy of the Home Owners' Loan Corporation." *Housing Policy Debate* 16, no. 3/4: 547–74.

Darby, Michael R. 1976. "Three and a Half Million U.S. Employees Have Been Mislaid; or, An Explanation of Unemployment, 1934–1941." *Journal of Political Economy* 84, no. 1: 1–16.

Engberg, R. C. 1931. "Functioning of Federal Land Banks." *Journal of Farm Economics* 13, no. 1: 133–41.

Ewalt, Josephine. 1962. *A Business Reborn: The Savings and Loan Story, 1930–1960.* Chicago: American Savings and Loan Institute Press.

Federal Home Loan Bank Administration. 1947. *Thirteenth Annual Report of the Federal Home Loan Bank Administration for the Period July 1, 1944, through June 30, 1945.* H.R. Document No. 44, 80th Congress, 1st session. Washington, DC: Government Printing Office.

———. 1952. *Fourteenth Annual Report of the Federal Home Loan Bank Administration for the Period July 1, 1950, to June 30, 1951.* Washington, DC: Government Printing Office.

Federal Home Loan Bank Board. 1934. *First Annual Report of the Federal Home Loan Bank Board Covering the Operations of the Federal Home Loan Bank Board, the Home Owners' Loan Corporation, the Federal Savings and Loan Promotion Activity from the Date of Their Creation through December 31, 1933.* H.R. Document No. 26, 73rd Congress, 2nd session. Washington, DC: Government Printing Office.

———. 1935. *Second Annual Report of the Federal Home Loan Bank Board Covering the Operations of the Federal Home Loan Banks, the Home Owners' Loan Corporation, the Federal Savings and Loan Division, the Federal Savings and Loan Insurance Corporation from the Date of Their Creation through December 31, 1934.* H.R. Document No. 31, 74th Congress, 1st session. Washington, DC: Government Printing Office.

———. 1936. *Third Annual Report of the Federal Home Loan Bank Board from the Date of Its Creation through June 30, 1935.* H.R. Document No. 337, 74th Congress, 2nd session. Washington, DC: Government Printing Office.

———. 1937. *Fourth Annual Report of the Federal Home Loan Bank Board for the Period July 1, 1935, to June 30, 1936.* H.R. Document No. 152, 75th Congress, 1st session. Washington, DC: Government Printing Office.

———. 1938a. *Fifth Annual Report of the Federal Home Loan Bank Board for the Period July 1, 1936, to June 30, 1937.* H.R. Document No. 515, 75th Congress, 3rd session. Washington, DC: Government Printing Office.

———. 1938b. *Sixth Annual Report of the Federal Home Loan Bank Board for the Period July 1, 1937, to June 30, 1938.* H.R. Document No. 90, 76th Congress, 1st session. Washington, DC: Government Printing Office.

———. 1940. *Eighth Annual Report of the Federal Home Loan Bank Board for the Period July 1, 1939, to June 30, 1940.* H.R. Document No. 46, 77th Congress, 1st session. Washington, DC: Government Printing Office.

———. 1941. *Ninth Annual Report of the Federal Home Loan Bank Board for the Period July 1, 1940, to June 30, 1941.* H.R. Document No. 540, 77th Congress, 2nd session. Washington, DC: Government Printing Office.

Federal Reserve Board of Governors. 2013. Z.1 *Flow of Funds Accounts of the United States.* http://www.federalreserve.gov/releases/z1/.

Field, A. 1992. "Uncontrolled Land Development and the Duration of the Depression in the United States." *Journal of Economic History* 52, no. 4: 785–805.

Fishback, Price, Shawn Kantor, Alfonso Flores-Lagunes, William Horrace, and Jaret

Treber. 2011. "The Influence of the Home Owners' Loan Corporation on Housing Markets during the 1930s." *Review of Financial Studies* 24: 1782–13.

Fishback, Price, Shawn Kantor, and John Wallis. 2003. "Can the New Deal's Three R's Be Rehabilitated? A Program-by-Program, County-by-County Analysis." *Explorations in Economic History* 40: 278–307.

Fisher, Irving. 1930. *The Theory of Interest*. Reprinted in 1970. New York: Augustus M. Kelley.

———. 1933. "The Debt-Deflation Theory of Great Depressions." *Econometrica* 1, no. 4: 337–57.

Fleck, Robert. 1999. "The Value of the Vote: A Model and Test of the Effects of Turnout on Distributive Policy." *Economic Inquiry* 37: 609–23.

———. 2008. "Voter Influence and Big Policy Change: The Positive Political Economy of the New Deal." *Journal of Political Economy* 116: 1–37.

Foote, Christopher L., Kristopher S. Gerardi, Lorenz Goette, and Paul S. Willen. 2009. "Reducing Foreclosures." Federal Reserve Bank of Boston Public Policy Discussion Papers 09–2.

Foote, Christopher L., Kristopher S. Gerardi, and Paul S. Willen. 2008. "Negative Equity and Foreclosure: Theory and Evidence." Federal Reserve Bank of Boston Public Policy Discussion Papers 08–3.

Ghent, Andra. 2011. "Securitization and Mortgage Renegotiation: Evidence from the Great Depression." *Review of Financial Studies* 24, no. 6: 1814–47.

Gordon, Robert A. 1952. *Business Fluctuations*. New York: Harper.

Grebler, Leo, D. Blank, and L. Winnick. 1956. *Capital Formation in Residential Real Estate*. Princeton, NJ: Princeton University Press.

Green, Howard W. 1934. *Real Property Inventory of the Cleveland Metropolitan District*. Cleveland: Committee on Real Property Inventory.

———. 1935. *Standards of Living in the Cleveland Metropolitan District as Depicted by the Federal Real Property Inventory*. Cleveland: Committee on Real Property Inventory.

Gries, John M., and James Ford. 1932. *Home Finance and Taxation: Reports of the Committees on Finance*. Vol. 2, President's Conference on Home Building and Home Ownership. Washington, DC: National Capital Press.

Hansen, Alvin H. 1964. *Business Cycles and National Income*. New York: Norton.

Harriss, C. Lowell. 1951. *History and Policies of the Home Owners' Loan Corporation*. New York: National Bureau of Economic Research.

Harvard Law Review. 1934. "Constitutionality of Mortgage Relief Legislation: Home Building & Loan Association v. Blaisdell." *Harvard Law Review* 47, no. 4: 660–68.

Hawkins, John, and Philip Turner. 1999. "Bank Restructuring in Practice: An Overview." In *Bank Restructuring in Practice*, Bank of International Studies Policy Paper 6. http://www.bis.org/publ/plcy06.htm.

Hickman, Bert G. 1960. *Growth and Stability of the Postwar Economy*. Washington, DC: Brookings Institution.

Hillier, Amy E. 2003. "Redlining and the Home Owners' Loan Corporation." *Journal of Urban History* 29, no. 4: 394–420.

Home Loan Bank Board. 1952. *Final Report to the Congress of the United States Relating to the Home Owners' Loan Corporation, 1953–1951*. Washington, DC: Home Loan Bank Board.

Home Owners' Loan Corporation. 1933–1935. Minutes of the meetings of the board of the Home Owners' Loan Corporation. Federal Home Loan Bank Administration Records. Record Group 195 and Entry 1. National Archives II, College Park, MD.

———. 1933–1951. Papers. General Loan Correspondence, Regional Office Correspondence, and General Administrative Correspondence, 1933–1936, Record Group 195.3. National Archives II, College Park, MD.

Jackson, Kenneth T. 1980. "Race Ethnicity and Real Estate Appraisal: The Home Owners' Loan Corporation and the Federal Housing Administration." *Journal of Urban History* 6, no. 4: 419–52.

James, John, and Richard Sylla. 2006. "Basic Yields of Corporate Bonds, by Term to Maturity, 1900–1975." In *Historical Statistics of the United States, Earliest Times to the Present*, millennial edition, ed. Susan Carter et al., vol. 3, 826. New York: Cambridge University Press.

Johnson, Thomas H. 1973. "Postwar Optimism and the Rural Financial Crisis of the 1920s." *Explorations in Economic History* 11: 173–92.

Lintner, John. 1948. *Mutual Savings Banks in the Savings and Mortgage Markets*. Boston: Harvard University.

Making Home Affordable Program. 2012. *Making Home Affordable Program Performance Report through April 2012*. Accessed on June 19, 2012. http://www.treasury.gov/initiatives/financial-stability/results/MHA-Reports/Pages/default.aspx.

Mason, David. 2004. *From Building and Loan to Bail-outs: A History of the American Savings and Loan Industry, 1831–1995*. New York: Cambridge University Press.

Mayer, Christopher, Edward Morrison, Tomasz Piskorski, and Arpit Gupta. 2011. "Mortgage Modification and Strategic Behavior: Evidence from a Legal Settlement with Countrywide." National Bureau of Economic Research Working Paper 17065.

Menderhausen, H. 1946. *Changes in Income Distribution during the Great Depression*. National Bureau of Economic Research Publications in Reprint. New York: Arno Press.

Mishkin, Frederic. 1978. "The Household Balance Sheet and the Great Depression." *Journal of Economic History* 35, no. 4: 918–37.

Morton, J. E. 1956. *Urban Mortgage Lending: Comparative Markets and Experience*. Princeton, NJ: Princeton University Press.

National Bureau of Economic Research. 1947. *Mortgage Loan Experience Cards, Roll 10: Home Owners' Loan Corporation*. http://www.nber.org/nberhistory/historicalarchives/archives.html.

Nicholas, Thomas, and Anna Scherbina. 2012. "Real Estate Prices during the Roaring Twenties and the Great Depression." *Real Estate Economics*, doi: 10.1111/j.1540-6229.2012.00346.x.

Olsen, Nils A. 1933. *The Farm Debt Problem*. H.R. Document No. 9, 73rd Congress, 1st session. Washington, DC: Government Printing Office.

Pennington-Cross, Anthony. 2006. "The Value of Foreclosed Property." *Journal of Real Estate Research* 28: 192–214.

Piskorski, Tomasz, Amit Seru, and Vikrant Vig. 2010. "Securitization and Distressed Loan Renegotiation: Evidence from the Subprime Mortgage Crisis." *Journal of Financial Economics* 97: 369–97.

Pro Publica. 2012. "Preferred Stock Investments, Fannie and Freddie Bailout." http://projects.propublica.org/bailout/programs/10-preferred-stock-investments.

Raskin, Sarah Bloom. 2011. "Taking the Low Road." Speech at the 2011 Midwinter Housing Finance Conference, Park City, UT, February 11. http://www.federalreserve.gov/newsevents/speech/raskin20110211a.htm.

Reading, Don C. 1973. "New Deal Activity and the States, 1933 to 1939." *Journal of Economic History* 33, no. 4: 792–810.

Reep, Samuel N. 1928. *Second Mortgages and Land Contracts in Real Estate Financing.* New York: Prentice-Hall.

Rose, Jonathan. 2011. "The Incredible HOLC? Mortgage Modification during the Great Depression." *Journal of Money, Credit and Banking* 43, no. 6: 1073–108.

———. 2012. "The Prolonged Resolution of Troubled Real Estate Lenders during the 1930s." Federal Reserve Board FEDS Working Paper 2012–31.

Rose, Jonathan, and Kenneth A. Snowden. 2012. "The New Deal and the Origins of the Modern American Real Estate Loan Contract." National Bureau of Economic Research Working Paper 18388, September.

Schwartz, Carl Herbert. 1938. *Financial Study of the Joint Stock Land Banks.* Washington, DC: Washington College Press.

Skilton, Robert. 1943. "Mortgage Moratoria since 1933." *University of Pennsylvania Law Review* 92: 53–90.

———. 1944. *Government and the Mortgage Debtor, 1929 to 1939.* Dissertation, University of Pennsylvania.

Snowden, Kenneth. 1995. "Mortgage Securitization in the U.S.: 20th Century Developments in Historical Perspective." In *Anglo-American Financial Systems,* ed. M. Bordo and R. Sylla, 261–98. New York: Irwin.

———. 1997. "Building and Loan Associations in the U.S., 1880–1893: The Origins of Localization in the Residential Mortgage Market." *Research in Economics* 51: 227–50.

———. 2003. "The Transition from Building and Loan to Savings and Loan." In *Finance, Intermediaries and Economic Development,* ed. S. Engerman, P. Hoffman, J. Rosenthal, and K. Sokoloff, 157–206. Cambridge: Cambridge University Press.

———. 2010. "The Anatomy of a Residential Mortgage Crisis: A Look Back to the 1930s." National Bureau of Economic Research Working Paper 16244.

Snowden, Kenneth, and Joshua James. 2001. "The Federalization of Building and Loans, 1927–1940: The North Carolina Experience." Manuscript, University of North Carolina at Greensboro.

Stevenson, William. 1933. *The Home Owners' Loan Corporation: Statement Relative to the Method and Procedure of Procuring Loans from the Federal Home Owners' Loan Corporation.* Senate Document No. 74, 73rd Congress, 1st session. Washington, DC: Government Printing Office.

Tough, Rosalind. 1951. "The Life Cycle of the Home Owners' Loan Corporation." *Land Economics* 27, no. 4: 324–31.

Urban Institute. 2010. *Metro Trends.* http://www.metrotrends.org/Commentary/mortgage-delinquency.cfm.

US Bureau of the Census. 1923. *Mortgages on Homes.* Washington, DC: Government Printing Office.

———. 1933. *Fifteenth Census of the United States: 1930, Population.* Vol. 6, *Families.* Washington, DC: Government Printing Office.

———. 1943. *Sixteenth Census of the United States: 1940, Housing.* Washington, DC: Government Printing Office.

———. 1975. *Historical Statistics of the United States from Colonial Times to the Present.* Washington, DC: Government Printing Office.

———. 2011. "Housing Vacancies and Home Ownership (CPS/HVS)." Accessed October 30, 2011. http://www.census.gov/hhes/www/housing/hvs/historic/.

US House of Representatives, Committee on Banking and Currency. 1934. *To Guarantee the Bonds of the Home Owners' Loan Corporation,* H.R. *8403* (S. *2999*). 73rd Congress, 2nd session. Washington, DC: Government Printing Office.

US Senate, Committee on Banking, Housing, and Urban Affairs. 2008. *Turmoil in U.S. Credit Markets: Examining Proposals to Mitigate Foreclosures and Restore Liquidity to the Mortgage Markets.* 110th Congress, 2nd session. http://www.access.gpo.gov/congress/senate/senate05sh.html.

US Senate, Subcommittee of the Committee on Banking and Currency. 1933. *Home Owners' Loan Act: Hearings before a Subcommittee of the Committee on Banking and Currency, United States Senate,* S. *1317.* 73rd Congress, 1st session. Washington, DC: Government Printing Office.

Wallis, John Joseph. 1989. "Employment in the Great Depression: New Data and Hypothesis." *Explorations in Economic History* 26: 45–72.

———. 1998. "The Political Economy of New Deal Spending, Revisited, with and without Nevada," *Explorations in Economic History* 35: 140–70.

Wheelock, David C. 2008. "The Federal Response to Home Mortgage Distress: Lessons from the Great Depression." *Federal Reserve Bank of St. Louis Review* 90, no. 3: 133–48.

Wickens, David. 1937. *Financial Survey of Urban Housing.* Washington, DC: Government Printing Office.

———. 1941. *Residential Real Estate: Its Economic Position as Shown by Values, Rents, Family Incomes, Financing and Construction, Together with Estimates for All Real Estate.* New York: National Bureau of Economic Research.

Winston, C. 1979. "Home Owners' Loan Corporation." In *The Story of Housing,* ed. Gertrude S. Fish, 188–95. New York: Macmillan.

Wright, Gavin. 1974. "The Political Economy of New Deal Spending: An Econometric Analysis." *Review of Economics and Statistics* 56, no. 1: 30–38.

# Index

Note: Page numbers followed by t indicate a table and f indicate a figure.